Managing Risks for Records and Information

Victoria L. Lemieux

INTERNATIONAL®

ARMA International
Lenexa, Kansas

Consulting Editor: Mary L. Ginn, Ph.D.
Composition: Rebecca Gray Design
Cover Art: Brett Dietrich

ARMA International
13725 West 109th Street, Suite 101
Lenexa, KS 66215
913.341.3808

ISBN: 1-931786-18-6

Contents

Part One: **Risk Methodologies—Risk Identification**

Acknowledgments

The author appreciates those individuals (regrettably too many to name individually) from Barclay's Bank, the British Council, and DuPont who commented on versions of the requirements-based records and information risk assessment methodology, as well as several unidentified reviewers who provided helpful comments on earlier drafts of this publication. Special thanks to Iris M. Fisher who worked through the methodology in order to test it and provide worked examples. The author is also very appreciative of the support and encouragement offered by the Publications Editorial Board of ARMA International, in particular Vicki Wiler, Managing Editor, Communications Department, who remained very committed to this project throughout.

Victoria L. Lemieux

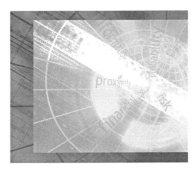

Introduction

Coping with Risk

In today's business environment, discontinuity, irregularity, and volatility seem to be the only certainties. The business world is full of risks. The environment, health, and personal safety appear to be under attack from hostile forces never before encountered. In the world of finance, new financial instruments turn up at a bewildering pace; capital markets exhibit growing volatility; global interdependence makes risk complex; and CEOs, directors, and managers increasingly are held personally responsible for corporate losses.[1] So, how do organizations cope with all these risks?

Because of the number of risks in today's business environment, risks cannot be avoided. Instead of trying to avoid risks, successful enterprises learn to manage them effectively. Failing to manage risk is the corporate equivalent of a rabbit caught in the headlights of an oncoming vehicle—doing nothing can be dangerous.

Risk management guru Peter L. Bernstein has written that "the revolutionary idea that defines the boundary between modern times and the past is the mastery of risk: The notion that the future is more than a whim of the gods and that men and women are not passive before nature."[2] Over time, humans have learned how to understand *risk*, measure it, weigh its consequences, and make decisions about how much risk to take on.[3] This practice has given rise to the science of *risk management*. A science, Bernstein argues, with the power to free humanity from fortune's whims and harness the power of risk-taking to achieve economic growth, improved quality of life, and technological progress.

Corporate risk management has evolved into a well-defined discipline. In fact, according to risk management expert Andrew Holmes, "The discipline of risk management has emerged to become one of the most important competencies within the

---

[1] Peter L. Bernstein, *Against the Gods: The Remarkable Story of Risk* (New York: John Wiley & Sons, 1998), 330.

[2] Ibid., 1.

[3] Ibid., 8. The word "risk" derives from the early Italian *risicare*, which means "to dare." This definition implies that risk is a choice rather than a fate. The actions we dare to take depend on our choices.

modern organization."[4] A recent special report in the *Financial Times* on risk management notes that, "Risk management has never been higher up the global corporate agenda."[5] By adopting corporate risk management strategies, any organization, large or small, private or public, can prevent losses and improve its business performance, quality of products and services, and safety. Indeed, risk management systems have emerged as a tool to complement existing management information tools and systems and can assist an organization to achieve predefined objectives and strategies related to core business functions, asset management, and projects.

Most large organizations, and many small ones, already have risk management strategies and programs in place. Risk assessment models and risk management responsibilities, procedures, and processes will vary from organization to organization, though they are likely to share common elements such as identifying risks and the likelihood and impact of their occurrence, assessing consequences, and defining risk control mechanisms.

Records and Information Risk Management

Although risk management has evolved into a mature discipline, records and information risk management is still in its relative infancy. As this aspect of risk management is still so new, no standard definition of it exists.

Records and information underpin every business transaction that an organization carries out. Any risk to the adequacy of an organization's records and information therefore potentially poses a threat to the effective completion of business transactions and fulfillment of organizational objectives or opportunities. The types of records and information inadequacies that may pose risks to a business include: (1) inaccessibility of records; (2) inaccuracy of data; (3) lack of credibility of information; and (4) incompleteness of records and information. These problems can originate with a number of different causes, such as natural disasters, employee tampering, systems outages, and weak controls, to name but a few. Typically, to the extent that businesses have focused on records and information risks, they have tended to focus on assessment and management of threats to records and information as part of business continuity planning exercises or information technology (IT) security initiatives.[6]

In this publication, *records and information risk management* is defined in a way that takes the broadest possible view of the topic. Records and information risk management therefore is defined as the management of any risk to the business arising from some inadequacy in an organization's records and information.

---

[4] Andrew Holmes, *Risk Management* (Oxford: Capstone Publishing, 2002), 16.

[5] Andrew Bolger, "Boardroom Juggling Act as Dangers Multiply," *Financial Times,* 1 October 2003, Risk Management Supplement.

[6] As an example of where current thinking on information risk management rests, see the interview with Peter W. Morriss, Global Head of Information Risk Management, and Andrew Street, Partner, Technology Assurance Services, KPMG, in Pamella Shimmell's, *The Universe of Risk* (Edinburgh Gate, Harlow: Pearson Education Ltd., 2002).

Purpose, Audience, and Organization

Managing Risks for Records and Information has three main goals:

1. To introduce records and information professionals to key ideas on risk management

2. To introduce records and information professionals and other readers to records and information risks and encourage them to take a more holistic and coordinated approach to the management of such risks within their organizations

3. To impart a methodology for assessing records and information-related risks

Why do records and information professionals need to understand risk management? The Meta Group, an information technology research firm, recently reported that by 2006 risk management will become a core competency for the corporate information officer (CIO) position. In addition, depending on an organization's industry and culture, between 5 and 20 percent of its IT budget should be devoted to risk management.[7] These findings signal that organizations are placing growing emphasis on the management of records and information-related risks and will therefore require the assistance of individuals with expertise in this area.

Records and information managers need to become key records and information risk management resource persons for their organizations alongside the resource individuals in other functional areas. Records and information managers are uniquely equipped to do so because of the knowledge they posses about their organization's records and information, as well as their understanding of records management tools and techniques that can help to mitigate records and information risks.

Many records and information managers, however, are unable to take on this role because they lack knowledge of basic risk management concepts and strategies. Thus, *Managing Risks for Records and Information* is written with a view toward helping records and information managers realize their potential as records and information risk managers by introducing them to basic risk management concepts, definitions, methodologies, and tools.

Part One: Methodologies—Risk Identification, therefore, draws upon risk management standards and the writings of risk management experts to introduce records and information managers to essential aspects of risk management. Part Two: Records and Information Risk Management offers high-level, but selective, coverage of common risk management topics, and it is aimed at launching records and information professionals into the world of risk management. The further readings in Appendix A will help readers who, having absorbed the basics about risk management outlined in Part One, want more detailed information. For ease of reference, key terms are italicized at first appearance and defined in the glossary—Appendix B. To aid learning, each section contains text blocks with helpful tips and key learning points.

---

[7] Nikki Swartz, ed., "Risk Management: A Core Competency for CIOs," *The Information Management Journal* 37, no. 3 (May/June 2003): 8.

Topics in Part One were selected on the basis of the author's assessment of their relevance to records and information professionals. Function-specific aspects of risk management—such as the management of market, credit, or liquidity risk essential to managing financial risks—were considered to be of marginal interest to records and information managers. In addition, some risk-related topics, such as IT security, are highly specialized and therefore this book—a primer on the topic—provides only an overview of these specialist topics. The use of risk management within records and information management projects also is not addressed. Readers interested in risk management as it relates to project management will find useful references in the further readings in Appendix A.

Part Two, which focuses specifically on records and information risk management, will be of interest not only to records and information management professionals but also to business managers, risk managers, information technology experts, auditors, and others interested in looking at risk management from a records and information management perspective. These individuals will gain insight into and knowledge of how to handle the unique challenges of managing records and information-related risks.

Generally, records and information risk management is not viewed as a coordinated and comprehensive area of practice in itself in the same way as, for example, operational or credit risk management. One of the goals of this book, therefore, is to encourage a more holistic view of and approach to records and information risk management.

Managing Risks for Records and Information promotes a view of records and information risk management as a distinct and coordinated area of practice, as opposed to a subcomponent of other risk management initiatives (e.g., business continuity planning or operational and legal risk management), which is so often the case. Treating records and information risks more holistically and comprehensively helps to ensure that possible risks to the organization arising from how records and information are created, stored, accessed, and disposed of are visible and proactively managed within a comprehensive framework rather than in a piecemeal fashion as a small part of other risk management initiatives. This approach can prevent important records and information-related risks or interdependencies between such risks from being overlooked.

Because an increasing number of organizational risks originate in how records and information are managed, a fast growing need has developed for a more holistic and coordinated approach to records and information risk management. In addition, their impact upon organizations' bottom lines appears to be increasing in scope and intensity.

Undoubtedly, the events of September 11, 2001, marked a profound change both in terms of organizations' awareness of risk to their records and information and the priority they assign to records and information risk management activities such as vital records protection and information security. Additionally, a sea change has occurred in the regulatory environment in which organizations operate. The

Cato Institute, a U.S. public policy think tank, notes that 4,167 new rules were issued by U.S. federal agencies in 2002 alone.[8] A number of these new regulatory provisions have to do with how records are created, kept, and communicated. These regulations were developed to address concerns about corporate accountability as well as the use, or misuse as the case may be, of personal information. Because the penalties for and other consequences of failing to comply with these new legal and regulatory requirements can now be quite severe, many executives understand the essential need to ensure that their recordkeeping is in compliance. The pervasiveness of information technology and organizations' increasing reliance on it has added to *information risk* concerns such as worries about loss or compromise of critical business data through system failure, technological obsolescence, or security breaches. In short, as organizations' dependency on their records and information has grown and the risks to those records and information have increased and become more complex, managing records and information-related risks comprehensively has become more critical.

To aid the comprehensive management of records and information-related risks, the second part of this book outlines and demonstrates the use of a methodology for systematically identifying, understanding, measuring, weighing the consequences of, and making decisions about how to manage risks associated with business-related records and information. The methodology may be incorporated within existing or planned corporate risk management strategies and programs, or used on its own. Presentation of this methodology serves to focus discussion of how the systematic assessment and management of records and information-related risks can be approached and applied not only to reduce the risk of losses arising from disasters, system failures, or security breaches, but also how it can be used strategically to assist the organization to operate more efficiently and effectively, achieve business objectives, and, as applicable, increase shareholder value.

This risk assessment methodology emphasizes identifying the risks to the organization if records and information required in order to transact and control business processes are not available or of the desired quality. In this way, it differs from most other existing approaches to identifying and managing records and information risks, which emphasize the risk to *records* and *information* from given threats. By identifying the risks to the business if required records and information are not available or of the desired quality, the central focus of this risk assessment framework is on the risks to the organization's strategic business objectives from weaknesses in records and information. The causes of these weaknesses may arise from any number of sources, including disasters, computer failures, or security breaches.

The advantage of this approach is that the strategic focus is never lost. The relationship is made explicit between records and information and achievement of an organization's strategies and objectives. This approach makes seeing the impact on

---

[8] Robert Francis Group, "Regulatory Compliance Will Drive New Financial Services Alliances." Available at www.rfgonline.com, accessed 03 March 2004.

the organization of records and information risks and justifying changes to and expenditures on records and information systems and controls that may be needed in order to prevent or mitigate these risks much easier.

Managing Risks for Records and Information illustrates the records and information risk assessment methodology with worked examples taken from field-testing of the methodology. In addition, Part Two also explains how readers can adapt the risk assessment methodology to focus on specific threats to records and information.

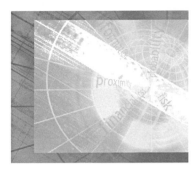

Risk Methodologies— Risk Identification

What Is Risk Management?

A logical place to begin a general introduction to risk management for records and information managers is with a discussion of the concept of risk management. An exploration of different definitions of the term presented in various standards and publications provides a window through which to gain a basic understanding of the subject.

The United Kingdom (UK) *Risk Management Standard* describes risk management as "The process whereby organisations methodically address the risks attaching to their activities with the goal of achieving sustained benefit within each activity and across the portfolio of activities." Similarly, the New York Federal Reserve describes risk management as "a coordinated process for measuring and managing risk on a firm-wide basis."[9] In his book on risk management, Andrew Holmes' definition of the concept underscores the systematic nature of the activity. He writes, "Risk Management is about following a deliberate set of actions . . . ." From these definitions, we learn that *risk management* is a systematic undertaking that involves assessing and addressing various risks to organizational activities.

Holmes makes some additional points worth noting about risk management. He writes that risk management is ". . . designed to identify, quantify, manage, and then monitor those things, events, or actions that could lead to financial loss."[10] Financial loss is always the bottom line in any discussion of corporate risk, but it may come about as a result of other losses such as major damage to buildings or systems, loss of a legal case, or damage to a company's reputation.

Risk management is also about being proactive. Dan Borge, managing director and partner at Bankers Trust, states: "Risk means being exposed to the possibility of a bad outcome . . . . Risk management means taking deliberate action to shift the odds in your favour—increasing the odds of good outcomes and reducing the odds of bad outcomes."[11] Borge's comments on risk management reveal that its goal is to analyze the business and corporate environment to assess threats realistically and take steps to

---

[9] Shimmell, *The Universe of Risk*, 5.

[10] Holmes, *Risk Management*, 6.

[11] Ibid.

neutralize or diminish them, rather than go blithely along hoping for the best. KPMG executives share this view of risk management and maintain that risk management is "about taking risks knowingly, not unwittingly."[12]

Risk management also is as much about identifying opportunities as about avoiding losses. Ernst & Young executives believe that "Business risk arises as much from the possibility that opportunities won't be realized as it does from the possibility that threats will materialize."[13] KPMG executives observe that, "An effective risk management structure allows an organization to understand the risks [associated with any initiative] and take informed decisions on whether and how the risks should be managed ... risk management is about how an organization can better understand its risks to improve its performance and deliver objectives."[14] In a similar vein, the UK *Risk Management Standard* states that the objective of risk management is "to add maximum sustainable value to all activities of the organization. It marshals the understanding of the potential upside and downside of all those factors that can affect the organisation. It increases the probability of success and reduces the probability of failure and the uncertainty of achieving the organisation's overall objectives."[15] In this book, risk management is addressed from both perspectives; that is, from the perspective of loss avoidance—for example in the discussion of the use of risk management to protect a business against the loss of its vital records in the event of a disaster—and from the perspective of capitalizing on opportunities—as, for example, in the treatment of the use of risk management for the purposes of managing information strategically.

From this brief exploration of selected definitions of risk management, the basic ideas of the subject are summarized in the key learning points.

For a deeper understanding of risk management, readers may continue their exploration with the additional readings listing in Appendix A.

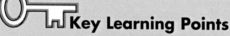

Key Learning Points

Risk management is:

- A systematic process comprised of a deliberate set of actions required to identify and control exposure to risk.
- A proactive process for handling risks.
- A decision support tool.
- A process aimed at preventing loss and capitalizing on opportunities to improve the operations of the organization.

What Is Risk?

At its most basic, risk management is all about managing risk. Risk management expert H. F. Kloman writes that, "Risk, like Sir Winston Churchill's description of Russia, is 'a riddle wrapped in a mystery inside an enigma.'"[16] So, how do we get to

---

[12] Shimmell, *The Universe of Risk*, 5.

[13] Ibid.

[14] Ibid.

[15] UK Institute of Risk Management (IRM), The Association of Insurance and Risk Managers (AIRMIC), and ALARM The National Forum for Risk Management in the Public Sector, *Risk Management Standard* (London: AIRMIC, ALARM, IRM, 2002), 2. This publication is referred to hereafter as the UK *Risk Management Standard*.

[16] H. F. Kloman, "The Risk Spectrum," *Risk Management Reports*. Available at www.riskreports.com/spectrum.html, accessed 03 March 2004.

the bottom of what risk means? As in the previous section, one approach is to review definitions of risk found in various standards and publications. From these definitions one can piece together some essential ideas about risk.

Referring to Andrew Holmes' definition of risk management, (remember that he refers to risk management as being ". . . designed to identify, quantify, manage, and then monitor those things, events, or actions that could lead to financial loss."[17]), we come to the understanding that a risk can be a thing, an event, or an action. Risk management literature commonly focuses on the *risk event.*

The Standards Australia risk management Web site (www.standards.com.au) states: "Risk is in essence a description of an event that has not occurred but has some likelihood of occurring." This definition introduces the notion that risk is about the probability of an event. *Probability,* or the likelihood that a risk will occur, is a key concept in any discussion of risk, and it is addressed in greater detail later in the discussion.

The International Organization for Standardization (ISO) standard for risk management vocabulary (ISO/IEC Guide 73:2002) defines risk "as the combination of the probability of an event and its consequences."[18] In addition to the idea of probability, then, in this definition the concept of *consequence* or *impact,* which is another key risk-related concept, is introduced.

Assessing the probability and impact of risk is a tricky business. It requires judgment and making assumptions about the future.[19] As Andrew Holmes has observed:

> . . . whereas assessing the likelihood of a road accident is quite easy, assessing the risk of nuclear meltdown is very difficult. This is because in the case of road accidents, there is plenty of information available against which risk can be assessed, but in the nuclear meltdown case there is very little. This separates risk (which can be managed) from uncertainty (which generally cannot be managed without the construction of theoretical models).[20]

Though making assumptions about the future in order to calculate probability and impact is difficult, it is not impossible. The "how" of assessing probability and impact is discussed more fully later in Part One. The bottom line is that risk can be managed.

Risk is also context dependent. An event that is risky in one business context may not be in another. Similarly, what is considered to be a risk in one instance may be thought of as a consequence in another.[21] The Turnbull Report on UK corporate governance states that:

> . . . a company's objectives, its internal organisation and the environment which it operates in are continually evolving and as a result the risks it faces

---

[17] Holmes, *Risk Management*, 6.

[18] UK *Risk Management Standard*, 2.

[19] Holmes, *Risk Management*, 6.

[20] Ibid.

[21] A 2002 article by Ian Abrahams on approaches to risk profiling defines a consequence as a measure of the cost after the risk event is triggered ["2002-05-28 - Approaches to Risk Profiling," accessed at www.riskmanagement.com.au/RM/NEWS/2002-05-28APPROACHESTORISKPROFILING, 26 August 2002 (hereafter referred to as the Australian Risk Management Portal Approaches to Risk Profiling). This article is no longer available online; however, the portal archives, available at www.riskmanagement.com.au/NEWS-ROOM/NEWS%20RELEASE/, includes other useful news items and articles about risk management.].

are continually changing. A sound system of control therefore depends on a thorough and regular evaluation of the nature and extent of the risk to which the company is exposed.[22]

For this reason, risk assessments must be undertaken within an organizational context. As Anne Kenney and Nancy McGovern, who are involved in Cornell University's Project PRISM on preservation risks to digital records, put it: "Each institution will need to define its own 'worry radius.'"[23] An organization's *worry radius* is the context of what defines perceived risk and acceptable loss. Some examples of context to bear in mind include:[24]

- Organization
- Division or business unit
- Functions
- Projects
- Assets
- Objectives and strategies

Key Learning Points

- Risk is a description of a thing, event, or action that has not yet occurred.
- That thing, event, or action has a certain probability of occurring.
- A risk has a consequence or impact after it has occurred.
- Determination of probability and impact requires making assumptions about the future.
- Risk is a relative concept—assumptions about the future need to be made within an organizational context.
- Risk can be managed.

Contexts can be mixed into combinations to create different risk profiles. For example:

- A business unit manages some building assets that require regular maintenance work
- A project has several phases, each with their respective functions/tasks to be performed

So, what picture of risk can be formed from the various definitions of risk found in standards and the observations of experts on risk management? Review the key learning points.

Identifying Sources of Risk

Generally, personal experiences and perspectives dominate one's views on the potential sources, or causes, of risk. As Christopher Culp observes, "Almost by definition, the risks that are the most insidious for a company are those risks to which it is exposed that have *not* been identified."[25] Before September 11, 2001, acts of terrorism

---

[22] Turnbull Report quoted in United Kingdom, Office of Government Commerce, *Management of Risk: Guidance for Practitioners* (London: The Stationary Office, 2002).

[23] Anne R. Kenney et al., "Preservation Risk Management for Web Resources," *D-Lib Magazine* 8, no. 1 (January 2002). Available at www.dlib.org/dlib/january02/kenney/01kenney.html, accessed 04 March 2004.

[24] Australian Risk Management Portal Approaches to Risk Profiling. No longer available online.

[25] Christopher L. Culp, *The Risk Management Process* (NY: John Wiley & Sons, 2001), 210.

on the scale of what happened to the World Trade Center were probably not on most organizations' risk radar screen. Unfortunately, acts of terrorism are probably now well within many organizations' worry radius. The future cannot be known with certainty; therefore, organizations need to consider a range of possible scenarios.

To help eliminate possible limitations of an individual's or an organization's executives' particular perspectives on the potential causes of risk and to stimulate thinking about possible sources of risk, the following models summarize the possible triggers of risk.

H. F. Kloman has developed a diagram summarizing his views on all major causes of risk, which he subdivides into two broad categories: global risks and organizational risks (see Figure 1). Global risks, according to Kloman, describe uncertainties that are seldom manageable but which have significant strategic effects.[26] Organizational risks, on the other hand, are more susceptible to control, according to Kloman.

The UK *Risk Management Standard* presents a slightly different view of the drivers of risk, dividing causes into two broad groups: externally driven and internally driven.[27] See Figure 2.

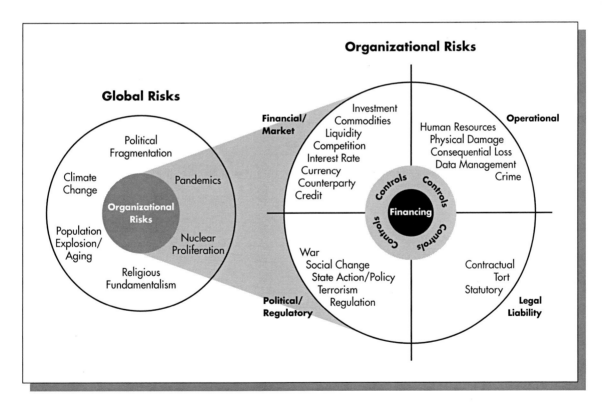

Kloman's Universe of Risk

Figure 1

Source: Reprinted with permission by H. F. Kloman, "The Risk Spectrum," Risk Management Reports, March 1998. Available at www.riskreports.com/spectrum.html.

[26] Kloman, "The Risk Spectrum."

[27] UK *Risk Management Standard*, 3.

UK *Risk Management Standard's* Universe of Risk

Figure 2

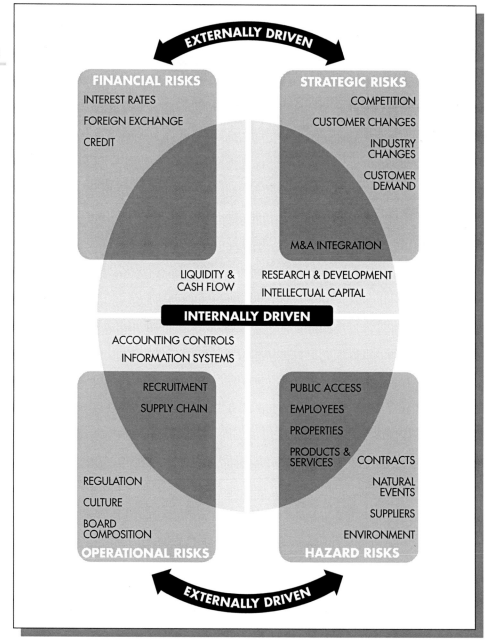

Figures 1 and 2 present only two views of the numerous causes of risk. Though neither of these views is definitive, they can at least serve to stimulate thinking about the potential drivers of risk in a particular business context, whether the risk is to an entire organization, to a specific division or department, or to a project. Once the

Tip

Concentrating on risk (e.g., loss of information) can work better if performing a strategic information risk analysis. Focusing on cause or threat (e.g., fire, water leak, sabotage, etc.) may work better when undertaking a loss-oriented risk assessment, as when doing disaster planning, because recovery strategies may be more dependent upon the source of the risk.

Key Learning Points

- Risk has many potential sources.
- Your view of the sources of risk will reflect your own experiences and perceptions.
- Potential sources of risk in your business context and your organization's risk tolerance level define your worry radius.
- A risk may have more than one cause.

worry radius has been identified, then one can begin to think about the probability of a given cause occurring and, in the event that it does, its likely impact.

A complicating factor is that a risk may have more than one cause. In other words, several causes may result in the same sort of risk. In a given organizational context, loss of valuable corporate information—the risk—may result from flooding, fire, or deliberate employee tampering with records and information systems—the causes. Thus, the relationship between risk and cause may be one-to-one or one-to-many. When performing a risk assessment, then, managers will need to decide whether to focus on causes or risks. One way to resolve this question is to treat each risk with a unique cause as a separate risk event, essentially establishing a one-to-one relationship between risk and cause.

The following key learning points provide a summary of the sources of risk.

Classifying Risk

Developing a taxonomy of, or scheme for classifying, an organization's risks is a helpful precursor to beginning a risk assessment exercise. A classification scheme can help ensure that the organization's risks are dealt with at the correct level within the organization and that suitably qualified personnel are involved with their management. The Project PRISM team describes *risk classification* as the process of developing a structured model to categorize risk and fitting observable risk attributes and events into the model.[28]

One way of classifying risk is according to its sources or origins. For example, the UK *Risk Management Standard* groups risks into four broad categories: financial, strategic, operational, and hazard. In this classification scheme, financial risks encompass interest rates, foreign exchange movements, and credit ratings. Strategic risks entail competition, customer changes, industry changes, customer demand, and mergers and acquisitions. Hazard risks, on the other hand, originate with the environment, suppliers, natural events, contracts, products and services, properties, employees, and public access. Finally, operational risks include regulations, culture, and board composition.[29]

Andrew Holmes takes a different view on the categorization of risk, grouping risks by their impact upon the organization rather than their origins.[30] His risk classification scheme consists of the following:

---

[28] Kenney et al., "Preservation Risk Management for Web Resources."

[29] UK *Risk Management Standard*, 3.

[30] Holmes, *Risk Management*, 6–7.

- Strategic Risk: Those risks that can affect the strategic direction and survival of the organization
- Business/Financial Risk: Those risks that can affect the financial viability of the organization
- Program and Project Risk: The risk that a major change initiative could fail or the benefits expected of it might not materialize
- Operational Risk: The risk that any aspect of the organization's business operations might fail
- Technological Risk: The risk that an initiative to introduce a new technology to the organization might fail

Other ways to classify risks include:

- By business function
- By their relationship to specific activities, for example, access to information
- By their behavior, for example, short-term impact versus long-term impact
- By their relationship to the phases of a project
- By whether they are idiosyncratic risks (e.g., one-time events) or systemic (e.g., subject to recurrence)

Tip

In deciding on a risk classification, be sure not to overlook the fact that the organization may have already developed a taxonomy of risks. Check with those groups or individuals in the organization most likely to be engaged in risk management activities such as risk management groups, business continuity planners, project managers, and the like.

Key Learning Points

- Develop a structured model with which to categorize different risks.
- Select the one classification of risk that best suits the organization's needs and business context.
- Be aware of existing risk taxonomies that may already be in use in the organization.

The previous examples of how risk can be classified are equivalent, but different, ways of looking at the same picture. No one viewpoint is inherently better than the other, though some will work better for a particular organization or risk management objective than others. Documenting the precise meaning of the risk classifications is important to whatever scheme is chosen. If classifications are not clearly defined, the terms can be used to mean different things to different people, which will lead to inconsistencies in the risk assessment exercise.

Although a preexisting risk classification may not be complete from the standpoint of records and information-related risks, it will provide a useful framework that can be expanded to incorporate any missing records and information risk elements.

Risk classification is a helpful step in performing a risk assessment, but take note: "Risks do not take kindly to discrete boxes, readily slopping over into one another. An employee mistake results in injury to other employees, damage to property (owned and others'), liability lawsuits, crackdowns from regulators and inspectors, and possible reduction in liquidity and the creditworthiness of commercial paper. All risks are interconnected."[31] All risk classification schemes are, to a certain extent, arbitrary. Pick the scheme that best suits the organizational context and the pur-

---

[31] Kloman, "The Risk Spectrum."

pose for which the risk assessment is performed, and apply it consistently. Review the key learning points.

Measuring Risk

As noted in the previous section, a risk has a certain probability of occurring, and having occurred, it will have a certain impact. Quantifying a risk's probability and impact allows management to make a more accurate assessment of the risk and better decisions about how to address it—the essence of risk management. In this section, the concepts of risk probability and impact and approaches to measuring them are discussed. *Risk measurement* may be defined as the quantification of certain risk exposures for the purpose of comparison to organizational risk tolerances.[32]

Probability is most often described as the likelihood or the chance that a risk will occur. Probability is usually assessed within a given time frame such as quarterly or within a year. Assessing probability looks not just at *whether* the risked event will occur within the chosen time frame, but also at *how often* it is likely to occur within that time frame. So, the frequency of a risk event is also an important consideration when assessing probability.

Risk proximity is another factor to consider when measuring the probability of risk. Proximity reflects the timing and duration of the threat of a risk. David Loader, author of *Controls, Procedures and Risk*, describes the notion of risk proximity in terms of a wave: Some waves are large and steep, while others are long and low.[33] Similarly, some risks may threaten at particular times for short periods, while others may be ever-present and continuous threats. Consider whether a risk is more likely to occur at a particular time, or whether it is likely to disappear at some point in the future.

Making assessments of probability can be very difficult because the future is a relative unknown. One of the best ways of assessing it, therefore, is on the basis of experience. For example, if you were to assess the probability of losing information because of a computer virus, you might ask, "Over the past year, how often have we experienced each type of computer virus?" The answer to this question would provide some idea of the likelihood of the risk that a computer virus will occur in the next year. If good historical data is unavailable, seek the opinions of experienced business managers. For example, ask whether they think the rate at or frequency with which the risk is occurring is on the increase (e.g., have incidences of infection by computer viruses been on the rise?), as the number of these occurrences may lead to an increased chance of experiencing the risk.

Impact has to do with the estimated severity of a risk once it has occurred. Very often, severity is measured in terms of *direct costs* or financial loss.[34] Direct costs are

---

[32] This definition is adapted from the definition of risk measurement offered in Culp, *The Risk Management Process*, 211.

[33] David Loader, *Controls, Procedures and Risk* (Oxford: Butterworth-Heinemann Finance, 2002), 83.

[34] Holmes, *Risk Management*.

the direct result of a threat acting on an asset.[35] They can arise not only from threats to financial assets but also from threats to other assets. David McNamee, in his article on risk assessment, offers the following ways to look at assets at risk:[36]

- Financial assets such as cash and investments
- Physical assets such as land, buildings, and equipment
- Human assets, including knowledge and skills
- Intangible assets such as reputation and information

This list of assets at risk provides a much broader perspective of the potential range of direct costs that a given risk may have for an organization.

Beyond direct financial losses, sources of *indirect costs* or financial losses must also be considered when assessing the impact of a risk. Indirect costs are related to the direct damage caused by a threat, although the financial consequences are not as a direct result of the threat.[37] Examples might include:

- Business loss costs
- Provisions for failure to identify and manage risks

Although a threat to an organization's reputation will not always translate into a financial loss, it very often will. For this reason, always consider less obvious factors when assessing the overall impact of a risk.

Assessment of these assets may factor in additional indicators of overall impact, such as the scope or the number of occurrences of the impact, as both these factors will contribute to the overall impact of the risk on the organization. For example, if assessing the impact of a disaster, a manager might look at whether that disaster affects the entire community (e.g., an earthquake, flood, tornado, or act of terrorism), is local to one building (e.g., a fire, water leak, or arson), or affects only a single department or individual (e.g., acts of vandalism, lost or misplaced files). Generally speaking, the wider the scope, the greater the impact. Similarly, the greater the number of occurrences of the impact, the greater the overall impact of the risk. For example, if a computer virus leads to a loss of information, more computers within the organization are likely to be affected, and therefore the greater the loss to the organization.

> **✓ Tip**
>
> When assessing the impact of a risk, review its potential impact on a range of assets, such as financial, physical, and human, as well as intangibles such as a good reputation.

Risk assessments must take into consideration both probability and impact. Risk management expert Christopher Culp explains the reason that both must be considered:

> Consider the risk that a comet or asteroid could strike the earth and wipe out humanity . . . there is some positive probability that this event will occur. But

---

[35] Peter C. Young and Steven C. Tippins, *Managing Business Risk: An Organization-Wide Approach to Risk Management* (NY: AMACOM, 2001), 92.

[36] David McNamee, "Assessing Risk Assessment." Available at www.mc2consulting.com/riskart2.htm, accessed 04 March 2004.

[37] Ibid.

does that mean everyone is ready to commit all of their personal funds to building self-sustaining caves in the ground below their homes? Hardly. Indeed, when faced with the choice between putting money toward a comet shelter or, say, keeping the local school open, concern about the risk of an event that could well cause the extinction of humanity becomes greatly reduced.[38]

Risk must always be evaluated in both probabilistic and consequential terms.

When measuring risk, risk managers usually assess *managed risk* or what is also called *residual risk*. Managed risk is the probability and impact of the risk giving due consideration to the controls already in place. Because risks are mitigated by internal controls, any such controls currently in operation will have an impact on the likelihood and consequences of the risk in question. Risk managers normally assess managed risk because the aim of risk assessment is to evaluate the effectiveness of the organization's existing control framework to determine whether the level of risk is acceptable and, if not, where additional or improved controls may be needed. Assessing the probability and impact of a risk without taking existing controls into consideration is referred to as assessing the *absolute risk*.

Having assessed the probability and impact of a risk, the assessed level of risk may be expressed in quantitative or qualitative terms, or a mixture of the two. A *qualitative risk measurement* includes assigning a ranking, such as high, medium, or low, to the probability and impact of a risk, based on a predefined scale. Keep in mind that the validity of the ranking will be based on the consistent use of a well-defined scale. Figure 3, adapted from the UK *Risk Management Standard*, provides an example of a

Sample Risk Measurement Scale

Figure 3

Scale	Probability	Impact
High	Likely to occur each year or more than 25% chance of occurrence	Financial impact on the organization is likely to exceed x
		Significant impact on the organization's strategy or operational activities
		Significant stakeholder concern
Medium	Likely to occur in a ten-year time period or less than 25% chance of occurrence	Financial impact on the organization is likely to be between x and y
		Moderate impact on the organization's strategy or operational activities
		Moderate stakeholder concern
Low	Not likely to occur in a ten-year period or less than 2% chance of occurrence	Financial impact on the organization likely to be less than y
		Low impact on the organization's strategy or operational activities
		Low stakeholder concern

[38] Culp, *The Risk Management Process*, 7.

qualitative risk assessment. A qualitative risk assessment could also be expressed numerically. For example, the high, medium, and low rankings could be converted into one, two, or three, with the same meanings still assigned to the rankings.

The advantage of using numbers over words is that measures of probability and impact can be combined to arrive at a single number to express the overall level of risk. The use of a single number is demonstrated in Part Two. Arriving at a single number to represent the level of risk can be quite handy, as using this number in relative comparisons of risks across the business or over time can be much easier. On the other hand, some organizations find that using words is easier. Different organizations will find that different modes of measurement suit their purposes best.

> **✓ Tip**
>
> Using a numeric risk measurement to arrive at a single number to represent the level of a given risk facilitates comparisons with other risks and of the same risk over time.

As stated previously, a *quantitative risk measurement* may also be used to express the assessed level of risk. For example, the value of the resources that would be lost if the risk were to occur is a quantitative risk measurement. The UK Office of Government Commerce advises using quantitative analysis only if the information forms an important support to decisions on responding to the risk.[39]

Figure 3, page 17, illustrates a 3 × 3 approach to risk assessment, in which both probability and impact are ranked according to three levels or grades. Using a three-point scale can make more difficult the decision of which risks are significant and warrant attention. For this reason, some organizations prefer to use a 5 × 5 approach to achieve finer gradation in their rankings. A 5 × 5 ranking approach is illustrated in Part Two.

Once rankings for an organization's risks have been determined, plotting these rankings on a risk map can be helpful (see Figure 4). A risk map graphically illus-

Sample Risk Map

Figure 4

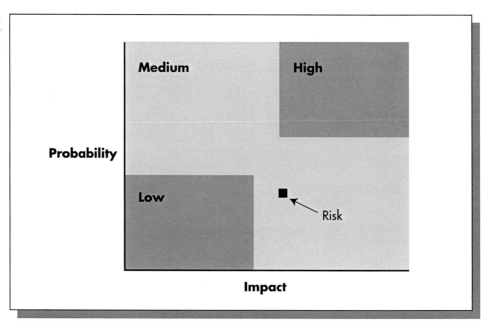

<hr />

[39] UK Office of Government Commerce, *Management of Risk*, 22.

Key Learning Points

- Probability is the likelihood that a risk will occur.
- Impact is the consequence of a given risk once it occurs.
- Risk management entails measuring probability and impact.
- Measurement of probability and impact can be qualitative, quantitative, or a combination of the two.
- Assessing the interdependency of risks is as important as assessing each risk independently.

trates where the risk sits in relation to the organization's other risks and therefore whether it should be treated as a high, medium, or low priority risk.

Bear in mind that measuring risks independently is important. However, assessing the interdependency of risks—the impact one risk is likely to have on another—is equally important.

Defining Risk Tolerance

The amount of risk an organization is prepared to tolerate, or its worry radius, will vary according to organizational context and business environment. For example, an organization may be prepared to take on more risk at certain times than at others, or to take on large risks in some operational areas and very little in others. Ascertain the tolerance for risk in order to know whether and how risks should be treated. Essentially, the *risk tolerance level* is the maximum exposure to risk—whether for a given type of risk for an organizational unit, or across all exposures—which is acceptable, based on the benefits and costs involved.

Risk tolerance can be defined in absolute or relative terms. These definitions will become the *key risk indicators*; that is, the measures that indicate the threshold limits of the organization's risk tolerance. Changes in the risk indicators will help alert management to potential unacceptable elevations in the level of the organization's risks.

An absolute definition of risk tolerance might be a specific amount of money that an organization is prepared to lose as a result of the risk.[40] Although absolute measures of risk tolerance are very precise, determining how much is too much can be difficult. A relative measure of risk tolerance is the level of risk an organization is prepared to take on over and above what it considers to be its natural risk exposure. This relative measure could be expressed as a percentage increase in the level of risk. Whatever measure is used, avoid any approach that is ambiguous or unmeasurable and ensure that it supports comparisons across different risk types.

Chris Frost, David Allen, James Porter, and Phillip Bloodworth, authors of *Operational Risk and Resilience*, believe organizations should ask themselves the following questions in order to understand their risk appetite:[41]

1. What risks is the organization prepared to take in pursuit of its business goals and where is the boundary between these risks and the risks it is unwilling to take?

---

[40] Christopher Culp gives some examples of how to define absolute risk tolerances in *The Risk Management Process*, 256. David Loader also presents some useful examples of how to define risk tolerances in *Controls, Procedures and Risk*, 67.

[41] Holmes, *Risk Management*, 110.

Tip

Once you have identified your worry radius, plotting it on your risk map can be helpful.

Key Learning Points

- The risk tolerance level, or worry radius, determines the level of acceptability of a risk.
- The risk tolerance level acts as a filter to ensure that time is not wasted on risks that do not warrant further attention.
- Risk tolerance can vary according to the business context.

2. Are the risks consistent with the organization's strategy?

3. Where should exposure to risk be reduced?

4. Is the organization too risk adverse and as a result missing opportunities?

5. How will the organization's stakeholders be affected by the risks being taken?

Avoiding all risk is both impossible and unproductive, but asking these questions will help an organization understand and define its risk boundaries. Any risk that is above the tolerance level needs to be addressed.

Developing Risk Strategies

Risk is not something to worry or be concerned about; it is something that should be managed.[42] A key part of managing risk is learning how to deal with it.

Organizations can pursue five strategies in dealing with risk:

1. Avoid it

2. Transfer it

3. Reduce its likelihood

4. Reduce its impact

5. Accept it

The optimum risk management strategy should balance the benefit of risk reduction with the cost of reduction at the margin, because beyond that the law of diminishing returns comes into play. As Christopher Culp explains, "It may be worth it to move from high risk to low risk, but rarely does it make sense to make the final step from low risk to zero risk."[43] Now let's take a look at each of these strategies in greater detail.

One strategy for handling risk is to take steps to avoid the risk completely. This strategy may result in the organization simply pursuing another course of action. For instance, if the risks of introducing new information technology are thought to be very high because the technology is still very new, then delaying introduction until the technology has been proven may be more appropriate. Avoiding the risk may not be possible, however. The law may mandate the activity that gives rise to the risk, the risk may be so central to the business that it cannot be avoided, or the risk may not

---

[42] McNamee, "Assessing Risk Assessment."

[43] Culp, *The Risk Management Process,* 8.

be avoidable in any real or physical sense. In such cases, management will need to consider other options.

Transferring risk entails passing it along to a third party such as an external service provider. Information technology risk, for example, can sometimes be avoided by outsourcing IT business processes to an information service provider. However, outsourcing a business function or process will not automatically avoid the risks associated with

Tip

Reducing the likelihood (if possible) that a risk will occur rather than trying to reduce its impact once it has occurred may be less expensive in the long run.

that function or process. In highly regulated industries, for instance, regulators may take the view that the organization itself is responsible for complying with laws and regulations whether the function has been outsourced or not. Similarly, an organization can still be held liable for failing to protect the rights of customers or clients if its arrangements with a third-party service provider are deemed to be inadequate or unsuitable. If pursuing this strategy, ensure that a solid service level agreement with the service provider is in place and that the level of service is monitored for compliance with the agreement—both of which introduce additional costs that must be offset against the cost of bearing the risk or pursuing an alternative strategy.

Strategies for treating risk also include reducing the probability that the risk will occur. In order to reduce the likelihood of a risk, focus on the sources of the risk or threats. Only through gaining an understanding of the cause of a risk will organizations be able to reduce the chance that it will occur. If management is aware, for example, that careless use of e-mail leaves the organization open to litigation, they can reduce the level of that risk by introducing policies and user training aimed at better controlling e-mail usage within the organization. This type of control is sometimes referred to in risk management literature as a *preventative control.*[44] Often, "nipping risk in the bud" through measures aimed at reducing the probability of occurrence is more effective and less costly in the long run.

Risk mitigation strategies aimed at reducing the likelihood of risk go only so far, however. Some causes of risks are simply out of our control. Nothing can be done, for example, to prevent natural disasters such as earthquakes or floods. Consequently, risk treatment strategies sometimes need to be focused on reducing the impact of the risk. Most business continuity planning measures aim at reducing the impact of a risked event once it has occurred. For example, computer hot sites are designed to bring an organization's systems back up quickly in the event of a system failure. These kinds of risk treatment strategies are sometimes referred to as *corrective controls.*[45]

One common method of reducing the financial impact of a risk is by means of *risk financing.* It is a strategy most often associated with the taking out of insurance. However, this approach is not applicable in all cases, as some types of risks may be uninsurable. For example, obtaining hurricane insurance may be impossible in an area that is highly susceptible to such natural disasters. Work-related health, safety, or environmental risks can also be extremely difficult to insure. Even when insurance

---

[44] Australian Risk Management Portal Approaches to Risk Profiling. No longer available online.
[45] Ibid.

is available for such risks, its cost may be prohibitive, making it a much less attractive option. Risk financing also may entail *hedging*, which is the use of financial arrangements to offset losses that may occur as a result of one risk against losses associated with another risk to neutralize the level of loss.

Finally, an organization may simply choose to accept a risk. This strategy is more likely to be chosen when the probability of occurrence and impact are relatively low, or when the cost of mitigating the risk is unattractively high. This decision can only be made once an organization has defined its worry radius in the case, what it defines as acceptable loss in the context of the organization, or its risk tolerance level.

Developing a risk treatment strategy will entail the following steps:

1.   Setting priorities for the treatment of the risk

2.   Deciding on the best risk treatment strategy

Tip

When treating risk, focus first on those risks above your risk tolerance line that affect a strategic part of the business and that have the highest probability and impact.

Measuring risks and setting the risk tolerance level already will have provided indicators to help set priorities for the treatment of risks. Focus on risks that are above the risk tolerance line, that affect a strategic part of the business, and that have the highest levels of likelihood and impact, as these risks indicate where either no controls are in place or controls are weak. In other words, these risks are the organization's high exposure areas.

Having set treatment priorities, choose the best course of action for treatment of the risk. To make effective decisions about risk treatment, first understand the nature of the risk (e.g., its causes and existing controls). Trying to reduce the likelihood of a risk, for example, that cannot be prevented is pointless. For each risk, decide:

•   Whether existing controls need improving

•   Whether existing controls need to be replaced

•   Whether controls are absent

Understand the business context to avoid wasting time on an inappropriate risk treatment strategy. For example, an organization is unlikely to want to transfer a risk if the regulators take a dim view of such actions.

When several strategies to mitigate a particular risk are possible, a cost-benefit analysis of the different options can assist in making a final decision about which control to implement. A cost-benefit analysis may be conducted in different ways, depending on the information available and the nature of the risk. Generally, however, start by determining the direct costs associated with a particular risk mitigation strategy. For example, some instant messages containing valuable information about the organization's business may not be accessible for future reference as they are being handled currently. Management might be considering limiting or banning the use of instant messaging in the organization in order to mitigate this risk, a strategy having no direct cost. Another option might be to introduce new software that would allow instant messages to be archived the same way that e-mail messages are archived, a strategy having a direct cost to purchase and implement new software. To carry out a cost-benefit analysis, consider the direct costs of each alternative.

After identifying the direct costs of implementation, compare the cost of each option with the cost of the losses that could be incurred if the status quo is maintained. Begin by asking, "How would the organization's financial position be affected if these instant messages were not available?" Would regulatory fines be a possibility, for example? If the expected reduction in loss exceeds the cost of mitigation, then the risk treatment strategy can be justified.

Even if a risk control strategy can be justified on the basis of a comparison of direct costs, it may still not be the preferred option if it negatively affects interested parties, incurs other indirect costs, or otherwise negatively impacts other areas of the business. In the previous example, for instance, management may decide that, although it is less directly costly to ban the use of instant messaging within the organization, it is not desirable because employees rely heavily on instant messaging to communicate with clients. To ban the use of instant messaging, therefore, may reduce the effectiveness of the organization's employees as well as incur indirect costs in the form of lost business.

For more information about conducting cost-benefit analyses, refer to William Saffady's *Cost Analysis Concepts and Methods for Records Management Projects.*[46] The further readings included in Appendix A also contain references to additional useful material on carrying out cost-benefit analyses for the purposes of risk management.[47]

> **⚷ Key Learning Points**
>
> - Organizations can pursue five strategies in treating risk: (1) risk avoidance, (2) risk transfer, (3) probability reduction, (4) impact reduction, and (5) acceptance.
> - Risk measurement will help you set priorities for the treatment of risks.
> - Effective risk treatment strategy can best be determined from a clear understanding of the nature of the risk and the business context. A cost-benefit analysis of the different treatment strategies may be helpful.

Adopting a Risk Management Methodology

Adopting a methodology or framework will help bring a consistent, structured approach to implementing risk management across an organization. Adopting a risk management methodology is important because, as Andrew Holmes observes, "Relying on instinct, gut feel, or raw judgement is never the best way to manage risk. The inherent danger of relying on this type of approach is that things will be missed, information will not be captured or shared, and risks will be either badly managed,

---

[46] William Saffady, *Cost Analysis Concepts and Methods for Records Management Projects* (Prairie Village, KS: ARMA International, 1998). A. Boardman, D. Greenberg, and D. Vining, *Cost-Benefit Analyses: Concepts and Practice*, 2d ed. (Upper Saddle River, New Jersey: Prentice Hall, 2001), may also be of use. In addition, Virginia A. Jones and Kris Keyes outline the annual loss expectancy (ALE) method of calculating costs in *Emergency Management for Records and Information Management Programs* (Prairie Village, KS: ARMA International, 2001), 34.

[47] See, in particular, Howard Kunreuther, Chris Cyr, Patricia Grossi, and Wendy Tao, "Using Cost-Benefit Analysis to Evaluate Mitigation for Lifeline Systems." This article contains useful case studies demonstrating how to conduct a cost-benefit analysis specifically to choose between risk mitigation strategies aimed at reducing the impact of natural disasters. Available at www.grace.wharton.upenn.edu/risk/wp/wplist01. html, accessed 10 March 2004.

or not managed at all. This makes risk management a lottery, and can lead to very nasty surprises."[48]

No single "right" risk management methodology is available; risk management standards and literature present many possible approaches. A review of different methodologies reveals several common elements, however. These elements include the following:

- Contextual analysis
- Risk identification
- Risk description
- Risk assessment
- Risk treatment
- Risk monitoring and control

Each of these common elements is examined in greater detail in this section. Areas of divergence between different approaches are also explored to provide ideas for consideration as to what will work best in the context of an individual organization.

Conducting risk management does not require sophisticated software or high-speed computers. The elements of a risk management methodology outlined in this section are intended to help managers structure their thinking and approach. As David McNamee points out, using a spreadsheet package or even sophisticated software can help with the risk management exercise, but it is more important to "get the thinking right."[49]

Contextual Analysis

Most risk management methodologies, either implicitly or explicitly, incorporate gathering contextual information—that is, information about an organization and the business environment in which it operates. Both the UK and Australian risk management standards, in fact, recommend beginning a risk assessment with an analysis of the business context and environment. According to the UK standard, contextual analysis entails gaining an understanding of the market in which the organization operates and the legal, social, political, and cultural environment in which it exists, as well as gathering information about the organization's strategic and operational objectives, including critical success factors, and threats and opportunities related to the achievement of objectives.[50] Pamela Shimmel, in her Universe of Risk Model, proposes that risk managers, in addition to gathering information about the financial, environmental, ethical, political, and social context in which their organizations operate, also gather information about the IT infrastructure, the information systems, the organization itself (which she calls "internal knowledge management"), the organization's external

[48] Holmes, *Risk Management*, 111.
[49] McNamee, "Assessing Risk Assessment."
[50] UK *Risk Management Standard*, 5.

knowledge environment (e.g., the media), e-commerce initiatives, and the legal aspects of the organization's operations.[51]

This type of contextual information is quite critical to the success of any risk management exercise. Here are a number of reasons for gathering contextual information:

- *To support the process of identifying risks and their sources.* Without a clear understanding of the environment in which an organization operates, risk managers will have difficulty knowing what kinds of risks the organization might be exposed to and their potential causes. Why waste time assessing the risk to an organization of a tornado or an earthquake if it is not situated in an area where these types of natural disasters occur? Similarly, unless the regulatory environment in which the organization operates is understood, managers may overlook critical regulatory risks that could cause costly losses if not addressed.

- *To help determine the probability and impact of identified risks.* Here again, determining the likelihood of a given risk to an organization or the impact it may have is difficult without an understanding of its environment. For example, if an organization is planning to expand into a new country, how are executives to know how likely the new office is to experience damage to its records as a result of civil unrest unless they do a little background research into the new business environment?

- *To support the process of identifying an organization's worry radius.* The ability to define what "acceptable loss" means within an organizational context requires an understanding of the risks. Gathering contextual information can help with this process.

- *To identify which risk treatment strategies might work.* Unless risk managers understand their business environment, they are unlikely to be able to differentiate effectively between the risks they can control and those over which they have little or no control.

- *To help set priorities for the treatment of risk.* When deciding on which risks to address first, start by treating those risks that might prevent the organization from achieving its strategic objectives, as these risks are likely to have the greatest impact upon the organization. However, unless risk managers have a thorough understanding of their organization's objectives, they will not be well equipped to adopt this approach.

Risk Identification

Identifying risks is unquestionably a critical component of any risk management exercise. Risks can occur at many levels within an organization, for example:

- Strategic level
- Program level

---

[51] Shimmell, *The Universe of Risk*, 99.

• Project level
• Operational level

At the strategic level, risk managers need to focus on identifying the key risks to successful achievement of the organization's objectives. At the lower levels, they need to look at the risks affecting programs, projects, and operational service levels.

Ideally, risks at all these levels within the organization will be identified, but the ability to concentrate on only one level at a time may be possible. One of the dangers of this approach is that, although a risk may materialize at one level, it may subsequently come to have an impact on one or more of the other levels as well.

Whether managers tackle one level at a time or all levels, the UK *Risk Management Standard* recommends identifying all significant business activities and their associated risks.[52] Andrew Holmes, on the other hand, recommends identifying only risks that can be managed.[53] This approach has the advantage of conserving risk management resources, as no time is wasted on analyzing risks that cannot be controlled. That being said, knowing whether a risk can be managed may be difficult until it has been identified. Identifying all possible risks against only the top ten objectives at each level may be a better way, therefore, to determine whether accepting the risk or trying to address it in some way is best. The decision about the best approach to follow should be based on the resources and time available and, ultimately, what will fit best within the organizational context.

Risk Description

Many risk management methodologies also suggest developing an objective description of each risk in order to display identified risks in a structured format. A description of each risk will ensure that the risk identification and assessment process is comprehensive, consistent, communicated, and auditable. Describing risks will help to ensure that the quality of the risk assessment data is high, which is a key requirement of an effective risk management program. It will also reduce the resources required to conduct risk assessments on an ongoing basis, because data simply has to be updated as opposed to recollected when the time comes to update the risk assessment. Finally, good risk descriptions facilitate sharing information about risks throughout the organization.

Identified risks are usually recorded in a *risk register*, which is a log that contains information on all identified risks. Each organization must

---

[52] UK *Risk Management Standard*, 5.

[53] Holmes, *Risk Management*, 8.

decide on its specific content requirements for each entry in a risk register. Generally, however, a description of a risk in a risk register includes:

- A risk identifier (i.e., a unique number assigned to identify the risk)
- The risk type (i.e., the category of risk into which the particular risk falls)
- The name of the person who identified the risk
- The date on which the risk was identified
- A description of the risk
- A list of related risks
- An assessment of its impact
- An assessment of its probability
- Possible risk treatment strategies
- Chosen risk treatment strategy
- Target date for implementing the risk treatment strategy
- Risk treatment strategy action owner
- Current status of risk and date
- Closure date

Tip

Be sure to keep track of the sources of the data used in preparing the description of each risk. This process will ensure that data integrity can be validated as well as assist in updating the data later.

Clearly, developing such detailed descriptions for each risk requires a great deal of time and resources. To cut down on these demands, the UK *Risk Management Standard* suggests giving early consideration to the probability and impact of each risk and fully describing only those risks with higher rankings. To save time and resources, also focus only on those risks associated with a more strategic area of the organization.

In addition, maintaining the data electronically in a spreadsheet, database, or specialized risk management software package can reduce the resources required to develop and maintain risk descriptions. Automating the collection of certain types of data, for example, via direct feeds from business systems, is another way to reduce the time and effort required to collect data on and describe the organization's risks.

Tip

The following techniques will help managers assess the probability and impact of risks:
- Dependency modeling
- Event and fault-tree analysis
- Real option modeling
- Statistical inference
- Measures of central tendency and dispersion

Risk Assessment

The identification of risks generally is followed in most methodologies by the measurement of risk, which entails assigning a ranking to each risk based on an assessment of the risk's probability and impact. This ranking will give managers an idea of the severity of the risk.

Michel Crouhy, Dan Galai, and Robert Market suggest the following guiding principles for risk measurement:[54]

- Objectivity: Risk measurement using standard criteria
- Consistency: The same risk profiles result in the same reported risks
- Relevance: Reported risk is actionable

---

[54] Michel Crouhy, Dan Galai, and Robert Market, *Risk Management* (NY: McGraw Hill, 2001), 491.

- Transparency: All material risks are reported
- Firm-wide: Risk can be aggregated across the entire organization
- Completeness: All material risks are identified

Risk Treatment

Deciding on the appropriate risk treatment follows the measurement of the risk. Before the appropriate treatment can be determined, however, risk managers need to evaluate the risks previously identified. The UK *Risk Management Standard* treats risk evaluation as a separate step in its recommended methodology, but in many other methodologies, it is simply part of the risk treatment process. Risk evaluation can be done by comparing the risk analysis with the organization's definition of acceptable loss—its worry radius. If it falls within the definition of acceptable loss, then the analysis need go no further. However, if it falls outside the definition, the manager then must decide how to treat the risk; for instance, whether to transfer it, reduce its probability or impact, or try to avoid it altogether.

Once the appropriate treatment strategy is identified, Standards Australia recommends taking a project management approach to risk treatment by assigning an owner to be responsible for each risk control strategy and setting deliverables and timelines.[55] This approach should include an estimation of the resources—people, plant, equipment, and budget—that will be needed to implement the chosen risk treatment strategy, which may already be decided if a cost-benefit analysis has been carried out to assist in choosing between several possible risk treatment strategies. The UK Office of Government Commerce advises that, whenever possible, plans to address risk should be incorporated into normal operational plans rather than maintaining separate risk management plans.[56]

Risk Monitoring and Control

Most risk management methodologies include some element of monitoring and control of the prescribed risk treatment strategies. The monitoring and control process offers assurances that appropriate risk controls are in place and working and that risk management processes and procedures are understood, being followed, and effective. An organization's risk monitoring and control process should:

- Measure that risk treatment strategies have had the intended results
- Monitor risks over time to detect increases or decreases in their ranking
- Monitor that procedures and information gathered during the risk identification, risk measurement, and risk treatment phases were accurate and complete
- Identify where improved knowledge would have helped to reach better decisions
- Identify lessons to be learned from the risk management process

---

[55] Australian Risk Management Portal Approaches to Risk Profiling. No longer available online.

[56] UK Office of Government Commerce, *Management of Risk*, 29.

- Assess whether risk management processes are adequate and being fully implemented.

Effective risk monitoring and control should include a reporting system to enable regular, upward reporting on the work done to keep risks under control.

Remember that no one right way to do risk management exists. Many possible methodologies are available and can be adopted. If the organization does not already have one in place, the records and information risk management methodology presented in Part Two may be helpful. The resources, particularly the UK and Australian risk management standards, outlined in the further readings in Appendix A also present a number of alternative risk management methodologies from which to choose. Risk managers are encouraged to adapt these methodologies to suit the particular needs and context of their organizations.

Key Learning Points

- A risk management methodology helps bring a consistent and structured approach to risk management across an organization.
- No single "right" methodology is available. If the organization has not yet adopted a risk methodology, the risk manager needs to select one that is best suited to the organization.
- Risk management methodologies have the following common elements: (1) contextual analysis, (2) risk identification, (3) risk description, (4) risk assessment, (5) risk treatment, and (6) risk monitoring and control.

Administering the Risk Management Program

Effective risk management depends upon making effective use of technology, processes, and people. Therefore, the way in which an organization's risk management program is administered is critical.

Traditionally, risk management has been the purview of a few within an organization. It was typically a function assigned to a finance or treasury director and, less often, internal audit, purchasing, legal, or even, occasionally, human resources. However, more organizations now have corporate risk management functions. These functions have, in the past, generally concerned themselves with such issues as insurance. However, they can now increasingly be found to be developing sophisticated risk management tools and methodologies. The IT department is another area that often takes on risk management functions. Even individual business units may perform specific risk management functions relating to their projects or programs.

The many arrangements for governance of risk management within organizations begs the question: Where is risk management most effectively positioned within the organization? As is the case with risk management methodologies, no one right answer exists. However, most experts on the subject of risk management emphasize two important points. First, a need exists to ensure that, no matter what the particular organizational governance structure, the risk management agenda is set at board level. As Pamela Shimmel writes, "The smart companies recognize that risk management is a board-level responsibility."[57] Risk management expert

---

[57] Shimmell, *The Universe of Risk,* 6.

Christopher Culp agrees, stating that " . . . to view *risk management* as novel, independent from, or even secondary to *general management* is to miss the whole point. If anything, risk management is first and foremost about sound general management," which is a board-level responsibility.[58]

Second, the risk management function must be coordinated, integrated, and enterprise-wide—often referred to as enterprise-wide risk management (EWRM).[59] Christopher Culp explains it this way:

> [EWRM is] a structured and disciplined approach [that] aligns strategy, processes, people, technology and knowledge with the purpose of evaluating and managing the uncertainties the enterprise faces as it creates value . . . It is a truly holistic, integrated, forward-looking and process-oriented approach to managing key business risks and opportunities—not just financial ones—with the intent of maximizing shareholder value for the enterprise as a whole.[60]

EWRM means that risk management must be embedded in the strategy and budget processes of an organization and permeate all its levels. In a global organization, it must exist at all locations and be highlighted during induction and in all other training and development, as well as within operational processes (i.e., development of new products and services). Though many organizations aim for an EWRM approach, few have actually achieved it.

Regardless of the risk management governance structure an organization establishes or has in place, the roles and responsibilities of each stakeholder must be clearly identified and widely communicated. Here are a number of ideas, drawn from a broad cross-section of risk management experts, about whom should be involved in risk management and what their roles should be:[61]

- The Board[62]
  - Drives the focus on risk management throughout the organization
  - Is ultimately responsible and accountable for all risks that affect the viability and profitability of the organization
  - Understands the extent and impact on shareholder value of the organization's most significant risks and ensures that they are managed
  - Understands the risk implications of board decisions
  - Encourages a positive risk management culture and appropriate levels of awareness about risk throughout the organization
  - Knows how the organization will manage in a crisis

---

[58] Culp, *The Risk Management Process*, ix.

[59] Ibid., 227.

[60] Ibid.

[61] The sources drawn upon for this section are listed in the further readings section in Appendix A.

[62] The UK *Risk Management Standard* states that an organization's board may fulfill its role through an executive group, a nonexecutive committee, an audit committee, or some other function that sponsors risk management, 11.

- Knows the importance of shareholder confidence in the organization and how to manage communications with the wider community
- Is assured that the risk management process is working effectively
- Publishes a clear risk management policy covering the organization's risk management philosophy and responsibilities
- Chief Financial Officer
  - Is responsible for all financial risk management activities
  - Acts on behalf of the CEO in implementing a suitable risk management architecture (though this responsibility may be the purview of the chief risk officer, depending on reporting lines)[63]
  - Is responsible for maintaining an effective balance between risk and opportunity
- Chief Risk Officer
  - Provides accountability for risk control decisions
  - Works with the organization to implement the risk architecture through which all risks will be managed
  - Ensures that the risk architecture is suitably maintained and updated when required
  - Monitors risk on an ongoing basis and manages and reports on the organization's risk profile
- Risk Management Function
  - Sets policy and strategy for risk management
  - Champions risk management at strategic and operational levels
  - Builds risk awareness
  - Establishes internal risk policy and structures for business units
  - Advises on available risk management tools and educates business units about their use
  - Designs and reviews processes for risk management
  - Coordinates various functional activities that advise on risk management issues within the organization
  - Develops risk response processes, including contingency and business continuity programs
  - Prepares reports on risk for the board and stakeholders
- Internal Audit Function
  - Is operationally responsible for the continuous assessment of risk within the organization

---

[63] Although in many organizations, the CRO reports to the CFO, Christopher Culp, in *The Risk Management Process*, does not recommend this approach because the CFO, by making financial decisions, can dramatically change the risk profile of the organization, which violates the principle of independence of the CRO, 235.

- Certifies the robustness of risk management data and methodologies
- Provides advice and guidance on matters of risk across all operating divisions
- Coordinates risk reporting to the board, audit committee, etc.
- Assists in the education of line staff about risk

- Legal and/or Compliance Function
  - Assesses risks from liabilities, new regulations, etc.
  - Advises on the design of legal risk management processes
  - Provides education to business units on legal risk management
  - Advises on and supports compliance monitoring of legal risk management processes

- Project and Program Managers
  - Manage those risks that can affect the outcome of their projects or programs
  - Ensure that any project or program risks that could have a significant business impact are raised with the chief risk officer or the chief financial officer

- Business Unit Managers/Directors
  - Take responsibility for the management of risks within their business units
  - Promote risk management awareness and objectives within their part of the business[64]
  - Have performance indicators that allow them to monitor their business risks
  - Ensure that risk management considerations are incorporated at the conceptual stage of any projects within their line of business and that risks are managed throughout
  - Ensure that any risks that have a wider business impact are raised with the chief risk officer or the chief financial officer

- Risk Management Committees
  - Augment the role of the other stakeholders by focusing on specific risk categories across organizational functions

- Individual Employees
  - Understand their accountability for individual risks
  - Understand how they can enable continuous improvement of risk management response
  - Understand that risk management and risk awareness are a key part of the organization's culture
  - Report systematically and promptly to senior management any perceived new risks or failures of existing control measures

As noted in the previous list of roles and responsibilities, one function of the board is to establish an effective risk management culture throughout the organization.

---

[64] The UK *Risk Management Standard* recommends establishing risk management as a regular item at management meetings to allow for consideration of exposures and to reprioritize work in light of risk analysis, 12.

Andrew Holmes stresses the importance of creating a culture that accepts and embraces risk because "Organizations can no longer afford to maintain a culture that blames, ignores, or sanitizes failure, as this prevents risks from being spotted in the first place, let alone managed and reported on." The board therefore must ensure that an environment is created that allows everyone to raise concerns and issues without penalty.[65] The following three important elements are needed to build an effective risk management culture:

1. A risk management policy
2. Assignment of roles and responsibilities
3. Allocation of appropriate resources for training and the development of enhanced risk awareness by all stakeholders[66]

An organization's risk management policy should:

- Be appropriate for the size and nature of the organization, its business, and its operating environment
- Be clear about roles and responsibilities for risk management within the organization
- Be clear about escalation criteria in relation to risk management (i.e., when to refer decision-making upwards)
- Ensure that processes and the culture/infrastructure to identify and manage risk are put into place
- Set up the mechanisms for monitoring adherence to the risk management policy[67]

Although in-house ownership of risk management is essential, outside consultants also may be used. Risk management professionals and specialists can provide advice on both the general aspects of risk management—including process, risk factors, and mitigation strategies—as well as detailed advice and guidance on specific categories of risk. Unfortunately, at this time, most risk management experts have a very rudimentary and limited understanding of records and information risk management. As a result of high profile cases, such as Enron-Arthur Andersen, and new legislation, such as Sarbanes-Oxley, however, the knowledge and understanding of risk management is changing. Nevertheless, using outside consultants can help supplement in-house resources when internal risk management resources are scarce.

The cost of administering a risk management program will depend upon the technical and organizational complexity involved, but it needs to be budgeted. The UK Office of Government Commerce notes that operational units typically need to spend between 10 and 30 percent of their budget on risk-related activities.[68] Risk management budgeting considerations include:

---

[65] Holmes, *Risk Management*, 111.

[66] UK *Risk Management Standard*, 13.

[67] UK Office of Government Commerce, *Management of Risk*, 7.

[68] Ibid, 16.

- Development, maintenance, and dissemination of the risk management policy
- Creation and maintenance of the risk management infrastructure
- Development or acquisition of relevant risk management skills
- Loss of business capability while implementing the risk management program[69]

Having determined a budget for the risk management program, executives will need to consider how to allocate the costs. Two approaches to cost allocation can be adopted:

1. *Risk sharing:* Costs are allocated back to the business in proportion to the level of risks generated

2. *Risk pooling:* All costs are absorbed at the corporate level

Either approach has both pros and cons associated with it. Risk sharing can be a powerful motivator to managers to reduce the level of risk they take on; however, it can be less than fair as many risks may be outside a given manager's control. In addition, if the manager never sees any of the funds saved, but, instead, sees the unit's budget shrinking, it can be a long-term disincentive to reducing risk. Risk sharing also can be difficult to implement. A number of years' experience may be needed before reliable data on the levels of risk faced by each line of business become available and, even when this information is known, matching costs to their risk source can be tricky, especially if indirect costs are also being used as a basis for cost allocation. On the other hand, risk pooling avoids these problems and introduces a level of budget stability not found with risk sharing, but it removes the incentive to reduce risk. As is generally the case with risk management, the organization should be aiming to strike a balance between the two approaches that best suits the organization.[70]

Key Learning Points

- Risk management is a board-level responsibility.
- Risk management should be coordinated, integrated, and enterprise-wide.
- An appropriate risk management culture is critical to successful risk management.
- A risk management policy that sets out roles, responsibilities, and key processes should be in place.
- The cost of risk management should be budgeted.

---

[69] Ibid.

[70] Young and Tippins, *Managing Business Risk*, 394.

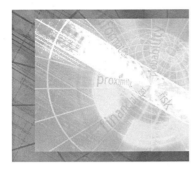

Records and Information Risk Management

Records and Information-Related Risks

Records and information risks encompass any risk to the business arising from some inadequacy in an organization's records and information. These risks can be many and varied, ranging from those typically addressed by business continuity programs—damage to or loss of records and information arising from disasters or major system faults, for example—to more systemic problems with records and information. Because the management of records and information-related risk has yet to be recognized fully as a distinct area of focus, no taxonomies are available to provide a comprehensive view of the types of records and information risks an organization may face. Tables 1 and 2, however, offer some examples of typical types of records and information risks. These lists can serve only as guides to the types of records and information risks an organization may face, as each organization will face different types of risks, depending on its business functions and context. The methodology presented later in this part will help an individual risk manager identify a particular organization's records and information risks.

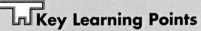

Key Learning Points

- Records and information risk encompasses any risk to the business arising from some inadequacy in an organization's records and information.
- Each organization will face different types of records and information risks based on its type of business and the business environment in which it operates.

Why Manage Records and Information-Related Risks?

Inadequate business records and information expose an organization to a growing array of risks from a wide variety of causes. In extreme cases, these risks can lead to heavy loss and even corporate failure. Recent high profile cases, outlined in Table 1, highlight how poor-quality records and information, and the organizational practices that lead to them, can expose an organization to risk.

Sector(s)	Primary Risk	Secondary Risk(s)	Cause of Risk	Consequence of Risk
Investment Banking	Legal[a] and regulatory risk	Financial[b] and reputational risks[c]	Failure to preserve e-mail in accordance with Securities and Exchange Commission rules	$1.65 million (U.S.) fine each against five investment banks
Auditing and Management Consulting (Arthur Andersen LLP)	Legal risk	Financial and reputational risks	Inappropriate destruction of records	Found guilty of obstructing justice Subsequent corporate failure
Utilities (Transco)	Operational risk[d]	Legal and reputational risk	Lost regional records of the number of gas leaks left for repair	Engineers waste time and money as they are asked to work on pipes they cannot find Health and safety executive investigation follows
Science and Technology (NASA)	Operational risk	Environmental risk[e]	IT obsolescence leads to disappearance of valuable satellite records documenting global warming	Inability to track global warming with potential long-term environmental consequences that are, as yet, unknown

Consequences of Failing to Manage Records and Information Risks[71]

Table 1

[a] Legal risk includes loss, damage, or unrecoverability of records and information that could result in litigation or non-compliance with laws or regulations.

[b] Financial risk includes loss, damage, or unrecoverability of records and information that could result in financial losses or threaten the organization's financial position.

[c] Reputational risk includes loss, damage, or unrecoverability of records and information that could result in damage to the organization's public image, confidence, or reputation.

[d] Operational risk includes loss, damage, or unrecoverability of records and information needed for completing the organization's business transactions effectively.

[e] Environmental risk includes loss, damage, or unrecoverability of records and information documenting the organization's environmentally safe practices.

The cases presented in Table 1 highlight the need for organizations to pay attention to records and information-related risks.

Aside from risk avoidance and control, effective records and information risk management can lead to improved performance of the organization. Records and information risk management initiatives are as much about identifying and capitalizing on opportunities to manage information strategically as they are about minimizing risks and losses. Some of the ways in which a records and information-related risk assessment can be used to enhance an organization's performance include:

---

[71] Carey Clifford, "Scary Records Management Stories," *Records Management Bulletin* 106 (February 2002): 18; U.S. Securities and Exchange Commission, Administrative Proceeding File No. 3-10157, In the Matter of Deutsche Bank Securities, Inc., Goldman Sachs & Co., Morgan Stanley & Co. Inc., Salomon Smith Barney Inc., and U.S. Bancorp Piper Jaffrey Inc., order instituting proceeding pursuant to Section 15(b)(4) and Section 21C of the Securities Exchange Act of 1934 . . . 3 December 2002.

- More effective planning of records and information management strategies and programs to ensure alignment with strategic business objectives

- Better control of records and information management costs

- Improved assessment and measurement of records and information management functions

- Improved decision-making in the records and information management arena

- Enhanced share value as a result of credible strategies to mitigate and manage records and information-related risks

- Improved compliance with records and information-related legal and regulatory requirements

- Higher level of preparedness for outside regulatory review

- Minimized operational disruptions

- Improved management information

- Improved knowledge sharing throughout the organization

Key Learning Points

- Records and information risk management helps organizations avoid losses and other consequences of poor-quality records and information.
- Records and information risk management helps support improved organizational performance.

Developing a Records and Information Risk Management Program

Failing to spot and manage records and information-related risks can prevent organizations from achieving objectives or can even lead to the types of business losses identified in Table 1, page 36. Failing to identify and manage records and information-related risks may prevent organizations from capitalizing on business opportunities. Few organizations, however, actually identify, assess, and control records and information-related risks in any holistic and systematic way.

In the current environment, where most organizations are very reliant on records and information and the risks to these resources are increasing in scope and complexity, failing to manage such risks holistically and systematically can handicap an organization. An ad hoc approach to identifying, assessing, and controlling records and information risks may mean that important risks remain unrecognized. This approach leaves an organization vulnerable to being blind-sided by such risks if they materialize. For example, J. Edwin Dietal, J.D., a U.S. attorney specializing in records retention, questions whether CEOs will be able to responsibly make the necessary certifications required by Sarbanes-Oxley if their records contain information content contrary to what they are certifying.[72] Similarly, important interconnections between business or control strategies for other types of risks and different types of records and information-related risks may be overlooked if less than a holistic approach is taken.

---

[72] J. Edwin Dietal, J.D., "Recordkeeping Integrity: Assessing Records' Content After Enron," *The Information Management Journal* 37, no. 3 (May/June, 2003): 44.

A decision to move business functions offshore may mean the imposition of new regulatory requirements for records retention, for example. If these requirements remain unidentified because the organization has not incorporated records and information risk assessment into its business processes in any holistic and systematic way, the organization may run afoul of regulators and undermine the strategic advantages of relocating offshore.

Despite the risks of failing to manage records and information risks holistically and systematically, records and information risks are not recognized as a distinct area of focus in most organizations and therefore no processes or people are specifically dedicated to managing records and information-related risks. In their book on risk management, risk management experts Michel Crouhy, Dan Galai, and Robert Market comment that, "Today it is relatively unusual to find sophisticated risk literate organizations with a decentralized risk management structure, where risk is managed to a minimum standard and risk assessment remains under the direct control of the risk takers."[73] This situation is not unusual, however, with respect to records and information risk management. In most organizations, line managers deal with records and information risks, where they address them at all, on an ad hoc basis through other business processes such as internal audit, legal, IT, or in some cases, records management. Their approach to managing records and information risks is purely loss avoidance oriented. In the Records and Information Risk Management Maturity Model illustrated in Figure 5, loss avoidance is the Ad Hoc stage of records and information management maturity.

In an increasing number of organizations, however, board-level and management awareness of records and information-related risks and the need to manage the risks are

Records and Information Risk Management Maturity Model

Figure 5

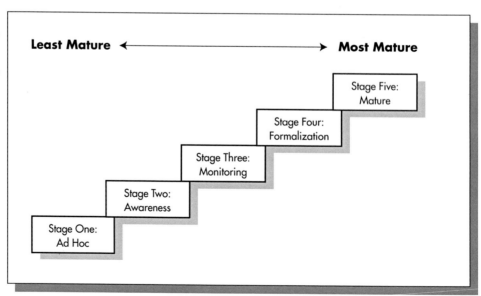

[73] Crouhy, Galai, and Market, *Risk Management*, 99.

growing. This awareness is likely brought on by recent high-profile cases involving records and information and new laws and regulations, though the awareness of the rationale for records and information risk management still is likely to focus attention on loss avoidance rather than opportunity maximization. In these organizations, personnel typically found within the business continuity planning, IT security, and legal functions perform rudimentary records and information risk identification, assessment, and control. Their focus is likely to be on the types of records and information risks typically addressed by these functions (i.e., disasters, major systems failures, threats to information security, and litigation or new laws). Other sources of records and information risk, if they are identified, are still dealt with on an ad hoc basis within each business unit. Ownership of those records and information-related risks that have been identified may or may not be clearly defined at the level of individual business units. In such organizations, the records management function, where it exists, usually still per-

Tip

What can you do now to move your organization from a stage one or two level of records and information management risk maturity to stage three and beyond?

Here are three ideas:

- Speak to other parts of the organization that may be involved or have a special interest in records and information risk.
- Engage with the rest of the organization to raise awareness about records and information risks through incorporating such awareness into existing training and development programs.
- Begin using a records and information management risk assessment tool to identify and manage records and information risks for at least some portion of the organization.

forms a more traditional role concerned with information retrieval or retention and disposition, though recognition of the need to widen its role to engage in records and information risk management may be growing. An organization with these characteristics is at the Awareness stage of the Records and Information Risk Management Maturity Model.

Managing Risks for Records and Information advocates for moving beyond the Ad Hoc and Awareness stages of records and information risk management into higher levels of records and information risk management maturity. The maturity model in Figure 5, page 38, presents three additional stages of development through which organizations are encouraged to move toward a more holistic and systematic approach to records and information risk management. The types of developments described at each stage of maturity are, at this point in time, largely hypothetical, because only a scattering of organizations exhibit any traits associated with stages three to five. The projected path of development therefore is drawn from developments in other areas of risk management, such as operational risk management, that have begun life in a similar ad hoc fashion and have, with time, evolved to higher levels of sophistication and maturity.[74]

One reason that many organizations linger at either stage one or two of the Records and Information Risk Management Maturity Model is often a lack of data within the organization about records and information-related risks and the losses experienced when those risks materialize. This lack of data may be because experience of such losses is infrequent, not tracked, or, if tracked, tracked as part of other types of risks and therefore not visible as records and information-related risks. One of the best ways of moving beyond the first two stages of records and information risk management maturity, therefore, is to begin to monitor records and information risk more effectively.

---

[74] Culp, *The Risk Management Process*, 434–435, was particularly useful in developing the maturity model.

At the Monitoring stage of maturity, the organization begins to view records and information risk as a distinct and unified area of focus. As a result, it monitors records and information risk much more closely and holistically. Records and information risk monitoring is carried out by personnel with specific records and information risk management responsibilities within existing risk- or records-associated functions (e.g., business continuity planning, IT, internal audit, legal, and records management). The notion of explicit and formal risk tolerances will have taken root, though measurement of risk tolerances is still likely to be qualitative. At this stage, the business also begins to track internal risk indicators using such tools as records and information risk scoring systems, such as the one outlined later in this book, and business unit performance measurements adjusted for records and information risk. Senior managers define their tolerances for records and information risk based on these measures.

The importance of records and information management as a risk management function as well as one traditionally concerned with information retrieval or retention and disposition also will have been recognized.[75] The organization will increasingly rely upon the types of controls traditionally associated with effective records and information management—records inventorying, indexing, retention scheduling, using procedural controls over records storage, retrieval, destruction, and the like—to mitigate the effects of and manage a wide range of risks. These controls will become particularly critical to the viability of the organization when the external environment is volatile, or if the enterprise is expanding the size or scope of its business or entering into new projects. Though the activities traditionally associated with effective records and information management can never completely eliminate all records and information-related risks, the organization's management will clearly recognize how these can help control the likelihood and impact of records and information risks.

Like any risk control strategy, records and information management strategies and programs can be costly to implement. For this reason, management realizes the importance of weighing the cost of controlling records and information-related risks against the costs if the risks are not controlled. A focused and systematic evaluation of risks versus benefits, whether carried out as part of a corporate risk management strategy or as a separate exercise, will have been adopted as part of organizational practice at this level of maturity.

In stage four of the maturity model, the Formalization stage, the organization adopts more systematic and formal structures and methodologies for records and information risk management. The organization would incorporate the concept and practice of records and information risk management into its business culture and risk management policies and procedures. The organization also would have developed a distinct records and information risk management function, which exists either as an independent unit or, preferably, within a unit devoted to enterprise-wide risk management operating under a chief risk officer. In addition, at this stage the

---

[75] Nikki Swartz, "Six Months that Changed the Face of Information Management," *The Information Management Journal* 36, no. 4 (July/August 2002): 20.

organization has developed a quantitative system for the formal measurement of records and information risk on a business unit basis.

The final stage of records and information risk management maturity, the Mature stage, is the point at which records and information risk management becomes a fully integrated part of an enterprise-wide risk management program. At this stage, quantitative records and information risk measures are integrated into other risk measures and reports, which may begin with the integration of records and information risk measures into measurements of operational risk levels. In addition, records and information risk tolerances are defined for the organization as a whole at the business unit and general levels. Finally, the organization has fully identified and incorporated records and information risk processes, people, and policies and procedures into its existing enterprise-wide risk management administrative structures and processes.

How should records and information risk management be administered within an organization that has reached the Mature stage of development? Generally speaking, records and information risk management should be fully integrated into the organization's enterprise-wide risk management program. This integration means that:

- Records and information risk awareness will be incorporated into the organization's risk management culture and policy
- Roles and responsibilities for records and information risk management will be clearly identified and will permeate all levels and locations of the organization
- Records and information risks will be highlighted in all training and development initiatives
- Records and information risks management will be a component of all operational processes (e.g., the development of new products or services)
- Consideration of records and information risk management requirements will be built into organizational planning processes such as strategy development and budgeting

Part One outlined best practice for the assignment of risk management roles and responsibilities. The following roles and responsibilities illustrate how records and information risk management should be incorporated into the risk management roles and responsibilities.

- Board
  - Drives the focus on records and information risk management throughout the organization
  - Is ultimately responsible and accountable for all records and information risks that affect the viability and profitability of the organization
  - Understands the extent and impact on shareholder value of the organization's most significant records and information risks and ensures that they are managed
  - Understands the records and information risk implications of board decisions

- Encourages a positive approach to records and information risk as part of a broader positive risk management culture and appropriate levels of awareness about such risks throughout the organization
- Is assured that the records and information risk management process is working effectively
- Publishes a clear risk management policy that addresses records and information risks

- Chief Financial Officer
  - Is responsible for understanding the financial implications of records and information risks and ensures that these risks are kept to acceptable levels
- Chief Risk Officer
  - Provides accountability for risk control decisions, including those relating to records and information risks
  - Works with the organization to implement the risk architecture through which all risks will be managed
  - Ensures that the risk architecture is suitably maintained and updated when required
  - Monitors risk, including records and information risk, on an ongoing basis and manages and reports on the organization's risk profile
- Risk Management Function
  - Sets policy and strategy for risk management, including records and information risk
  - Champions records and information risk management at strategic and operational levels
  - Builds records and information risk awareness
  - Establishes internal risk policy that addresses records and information risk along with other risk types and structures for business units
  - Advises on available records and information risk management tools and educates business units about their use
  - Designs and reviews processes for records and information risk management
  - Coordinates various functional activities that advise on risk management issues, including records and information risk management, within the organization
  - Develops risk response processes, including for records and information risk management
  - Prepares reports on risk, including records and information risk management, for the board and stakeholders
- Internal Audit Function
  - Is operationally responsible for the continuous assessment of risk, including records and information risk, within the organization

- Certifies the robustness of records and information risk management data and methodologies
- Provides advice and guidance on matters of records and information risk across all operating divisions
- Assists in the education of line staff about records and information risk

- Legal and/or Compliance Function
  - Assesses records and information risks from liabilities, new regulations, etc.
  - Advises on records-related legal and regulatory requirements
  - Provides education to business units on legal and regulatory records and information risk management requirements in collaboration with other functional areas (e.g., records management)
  - Advises on and supports compliance monitoring of legal and regulatory records and information risk management requirements

- Records Management Function
  - Assists the risk management function and the rest of the organization to understand and identify records and information risks
  - Collaborates with the risk management function to set policy and strategy for records and information risk management
  - Collaborates in the identification and implementation of records and information management risk responses

- IT Function
  - Assists the risk management function and the rest of the organization to understand and identify records and information risks
  - Collaborates with the risk management function to set policy and strategy for records and information risk management
  - Collaborates in the identification and implementation of records and information management risk responses, in particular, by providing an appropriate technology infrastructure to monitor and control records and information risk

- Project and Program Managers
  - Actively manage those records and information risks that can affect the outcome of their projects or programs
  - Ensure that any records and information risks that could have a significant business impact are raised with the chief risk officer or chief financial officer

- Business Unit Managers/Directors
  - Take responsibility for the management of records and information risks within their business units
  - Promote records and information risk management awareness and objectives within their part of the business
  - Have performance indicators that allow them to monitor their business risks, including those associated with records and information

- Ensure that any records and information risks that have a wider business impact are raised with the chief risk officer
- Records and Information Risk Management Committee
  - Augments the role of the other stakeholders by focusing specifically on the records and information risk category across all organizational functions
- Individual Employees
  - Understand their accountability for individual records and information risks
  - Understand how they can enable continuous improvement of records and information risk management response
  - Report systematically and promptly to senior management any perceived new records and information risks or failures of existing control measures

Key Learning Points

- Records and information risks should be managed in a holistic and systematic manner.
- Development of a records and information risk management program includes five stages:
  1. Ad hoc – Records and information risk carried out in an ad hoc fashion.
  2. Awareness – Organization becomes aware of the need to undertake records and information risk management as a distinct area of focus.
  3. Monitoring – Organization begins to monitor records and information risks at the business unit level.
  4. Formalizing – Organization develops more formal administrative structures and processes for records and information risk management.
  5. Mature – Records and information risk management is fully integrated into the organization's enterprise-wide risk management program.
- Most organizations have reached only stages one or two of the Records and Information Risk Management Maturity Model.

This list of roles and responsibilities reflects the incorporation of records and information risk awareness and management into existing risk management administrative structures, processes, and technologies. In addition, roles and responsibilities for functional areas that have traditionally focused on records and information management or dealt with certain types of records and information risk, such as a records management department or the IT department, will need to be redefined in relation to how records and information risk management fits into the organization's enterprise-wide risk management program. Finally, just as is the case with other types of risks that cut across organizational boundaries, administration of records and information risks may be aided by the establishment of a committee that focuses specifically on this risk category from a cross-organizational perspective.

Approaches to Identifying and Managing Records and Information Risks

Organizations traditionally have identified and managed their records and information risks by a trigger event or threat. Table 2 lists a number of common trigger events or threats to records and information that organizations typically take into consideration and aim to address as part of their risk management initiatives or programs. This summary provides an idea of the types of records and information risks an organization may need to identify and manage.

Trigger Event	Risk	Risk Mitigation Strategy	Owner of Risk Mitigation Strategy
Disaster – Natural or human caused (e.g., fire, flood, earthquake)	Loss or damage to records and information	Disaster preparedness and recovery program	Business continuity planning group and/or records management
Major system outages or disruptions caused by system or human errors	Loss or damage to records and information	System backup and recovery strategy	Business continuity planning and/or IT group
Computer fraud	Loss of funds	IT security strategy	IT security group
Theft of electronic information and electronic information assets	Loss of critical business information, potentially leading to possible loss of funds or damage to reputation	IT security strategy	IT security group
Theft of computer system resources (e.g., use of organization's computer systems for other than official purposes)	Loss of funds or damage to reputation	IT security strategy	IT security group
Malicious attacks and harmful code (e.g., virus attacks, hackers, etc.)	Loss of critical business information and/or funds	IT security	IT security group
Unauthorized disclosure of electronic information	Loss of confidentiality of business information, leading to possible loss of funds and/or damage to reputation	IT security	IT security group
Errors and omissions in documentation	Critical business information missing, resulting in an inability to enforce a contract and/or third-party liability, and possibly leading to loss of funds and/or damage to reputation	Documentation procedures	Legal and/or line of business
Inadequate retention periods for records and information	Records and information unavailable, resulting in noncompliance with laws and regulations and/or inability to enforce contracts or support litigation, and possibly leading to loss of funds and/or damage to reputation	Retention scheduling	Legal and/or records management group

Event-Based Records and Information Risks

Table 2

The traditional approach usually begins with a survey of the organizational environment to identify all possible sources of threats to records and information. The business impact of these risks is then assessed. The diagram in Figure 6 illustrates the process.

Table 2 identifies some of the risk mitigation strategies organizations typically employ to address commonly identified threats to records and information. In most cases in a large organization, management assigns ownership of these risk mitigation strategies to particular groups or functional areas. For example, business continuity

Approaches to
Identifying and
Managing
Records and
Information Risk

Figure 6

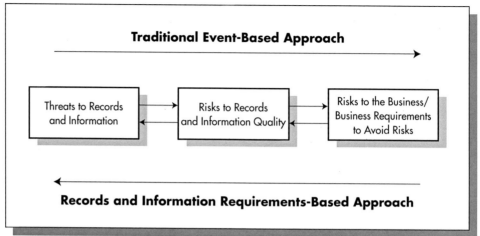

groups will focus on risks arising from disasters and major system outages; IT security groups will focus on risks arising from breaches of computer security; and legal
groups will focus on risks arising from laws, regulations, or litigation.

Another approach to identifying and managing records and information risks
is to begin with an analysis of the organization's business requirements for records
and information. For example, managers might ask, "What type and quality of
records and information does the organization require to support its critical business processes and transactions?" Risk arises whenever the organization's records
and information fail to match these requirements. Such requirements may derive
from laws and regulations as well as from organizational business needs.

J. Edwin Dietal, J.D., has identified some standard records and information quality characteristics that organizations may require of their records and information.[76]
These characteristics are summarized in Table 3. Not all these quality characteristics
will be needed to support the business processes and transactions of every organization. An organization may require other qualities of its records and information that
are not listed in Table 3. Similarly, the definitions provided in the table may not suit
the context of every organization. To adapt this approach, each organization will
need to assess the quality characteristics best suited to its business requirements,
develop consistent definitions for these qualities, and determine their relative importance. The records and information risk assessment tool outlined later in this part
provides guidance on how to undertake this work.

Having identified the qualities required of its records and information, the
organization then would assess the impact on its business if records and information
are not of the required quality. Finally, the analysis would examine the possible types
of threats or sources that could cause the organization's records and information to
fall short of identified records and information standards, and the likelihood and
impact of these causes.

---

[76] Dietal, "Recordkeeping Integrity," 44–48.

Quality
Characteristics of
Records and
Information

Table 3

Quality	Definition
Accuracy	Information that lacks simple errors in transcription, collection, or aggregation
Completeness	Information that is accurate and complete (i.e., no holes in the data)
Precision	Information that possesses the correct degree of precision (e.g., the correct dimensions of parts to ensure that they fit together properly)
Timeliness	Information that is not currently out-of-date, as well as the retrievability of the information within the user's required timelines
Appropriate for retention	Information that does not reflect circumstances now outside of accepted norms, reveal vulnerabilities, or raise the possibility of liabilities
Relevancy	The information's significance in the context in which it will be used and to the organization's business needs
Understandability	Information that is perceived to be clearly communicated and well organized by the user, or that which is cognitively accessible to the user
Adequacy	Information that is sufficiently detailed for its intended use
Credibility	Information that is perceived to be objective, unbiased, trustworthy, accurate, and complete
Reliability	Information that users trust and that, if used again, produces the same results
Ability to share	Information that can be shared among the people who can use it productively
Ability to engage	Information that captures the user's attention so that he/she puts it to use. This use is often dependent on format, medium, and presentation
Accessibility and retrievability	Information that can be retrieved when needed in a time frame that suits the user
Valuable and fitting	Information that contributes value to the organization
Reusability	Information that is available for use more than once
Affordability	Information that is worth the cost of creation or collection in relation to its intended use
Persuadability	Information that has the ability to persuade others of its accuracy, completeness, and quality
Communicability	Information that effectively communicates its creator's meaning (i.e., has clarity, simplicity, and completeness)
Potential to be needed in the future	Information that that may be used in the future

Both approaches—the event-based and the records and information requirements-based—to identifying and managing records and information risks possess strengths and weaknesses. For example, the traditional event-based approach may make identifying risk mitigation strategies easier because the analysis begins with a clearly identifiable trigger event or threat. The requirements-based approach may require more analysis to arrive at a risk mitigation strategy, as a number of causes are possible for poor records and information quality. Inaccessibility of records, for example, could be the result of inadequate indexing, technological obsolescence rendering the records unreadable, or unauthorized records destruction. Clearly, the risk mitigation strategies needed to address these causes will be quite different, though the resulting risk—inaccessible records—is the same for each root cause. For this reason, if time and resources are short, or management wants to address only a particular trigger event or threat, the traditional approach may be better suited to the organization's needs. The traditional approach, because it is widely employed, also may be easier to integrate with any existing risk taxonomy or risk management program the organization may have in place.

The requirements approach does have several advantages, however. First, because it begins with an analysis of the records and information requirements needed to support transacting an organization's business and attaining its goals and objectives, it can be a better method to employ when using risk management for strategic purposes as opposed to using it for the purpose of avoiding losses from particular threats. In addition, the traditional event-based approach tends to perpetuate a splintered approach to records and information risk management owing to the fact that, in many organizations, specific functional areas or business groups typically deal with certain types of threats. With the requirements approach, however, the process of identifying the risks starts with the organization's business needs for records and information, which may have the effect of promoting greater creativity and cross-functional cooperation in the development of risk treatment strategies. Finally, the traditional approach, in focusing on threats, tends to overlook more systemic causes of records and information risks such as poorly integrated systems, poor procedural controls, and the like. The requirements approach is much better at detecting systemic problems leading to inadequacies in an organization's records and information. Table 4 summarizes the pros and cons of both approaches.

The following sections present a methodology developed to assess records and information risks using a requirements-based approach as well as ideas for adapting this methodology to support a more traditional event-based approach. Choose whichever method best suits the organization's records and information risk management objectives and business context.

Key Learning Points

- Organizations traditionally have used an approach to identifying and managing records and information risks that focuses on particular types of trigger events or threats.
- An alternative approach is to focus on the types and quality of records and information needed to support business processes and attainment of organizational goals and objectives.
- Each approach has its strengths and weaknesses (summarized in Table 4).

Strengths and Weaknesses of Event-Based vs. Requirements-Based Approach

Table 4

Approach	Strengths	Weaknesses
Event-Based Approach	Easier to identify risk mitigation strategies	Less useful for achieving a strategic focus
	May require less time and fewer resources	May perpetuate a splintered approach to addressing records and information risks
	More useful for mounting a defensive strategy against a known threat	May overlook more systemic causes of records and information risk
Records and Information Requirements-Based Approach	Maintains a strategic focus	May be more time-consuming and take more resources to carry out
	Promotes a more creative, cross-functional approach to records and information risk management	May be less useful if focusing analysis on a known threat
	More helpful in identifying systemic types of records and information risks	May not be as easy to integrate into existing organizational risk management practice

Requirements-Based Records and Information Risk Assessment Methodology

No single best way is available to perform a records and information risk assessment. However, a clear framework brings a consistent, structured approach to the implementation of risk management across the enterprise. One possible framework for records and information risk assessment is presented next. The framework is designed to support a records and information requirements-based approach to identifying and managing records and information risks.

This records and information risk assessment methodology was originally developed because of a perceived absence of tools to help identify the business risks to organizations when their records and information failed to support the requirements of business functions, processes, and internal and external accountabilities.[77]

The framework consists of a nine-step methodology for assessing records and information requirements and risks. The steps illustrated in Figure 7, page 50, are as follows:

---

[77] An early version of this methodology took shape during a records management consultancy for Grace Kennedy & Co. Ltd. of Kingston, Jamaica. Over the course of many other records management consultancies, the usefulness of such a framework in assessing the records and information requirements and risks of diverse organizations became increasingly apparent. Subsequently, field research, ongoing consulting experience, and feedback from the staff of Barclay's Bank, the British Council, and DuPont on the usefulness and layout of the methodology have led to modifications and many improvements, though any errors and omissions remain the author's responsibility.

Requirements-
Based Risk
Assessment
Methodology

Figure 7

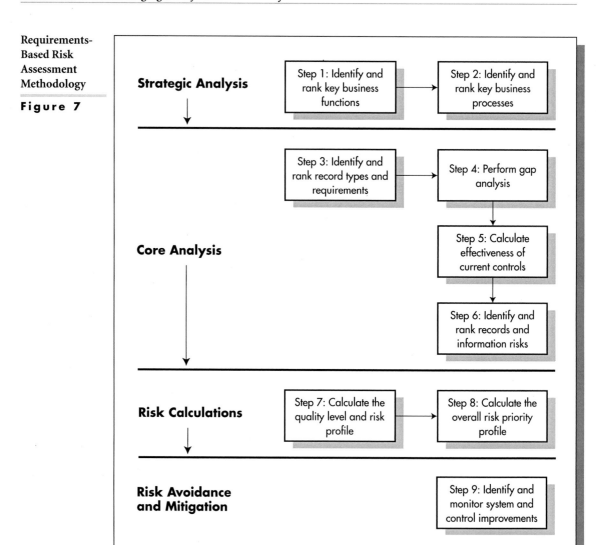

- *Step 1:* Identify and rank key business functions or strategies and objectives
- *Step 2:* Identify and rank key business processes associated with all or a targeted business function
- *Step 3:* Identify and rank the type and quality of records and information required to complete business process transactions effectively and to meet internal and external accountabilities
- *Step 4:* Identify the degree to which current records and information management systems and controls satisfy each quality requirement
- *Step 5:* Calculate the records and information systems and controls effectiveness rating

Key Learning Points

- The records requirements-based methodology for assessing records and information-related risks was developed specifically to help organizations identify the business risks that can occur when records and information fail to support business functions or meet internal and external accountability requirements.
- The methodology consists of nine steps (outlined on pages 50–51 and explained in detail in the following sections).

- *Step 6:* Identify and rank (by likelihood and consequence) the types of risks to the organization from gaps between quality requirements and the quality of records and information delivered by existing systems and controls

- *Step 7:* Calculate the quality level and risk profile for each category of records and information

- *Step 8:* Calculate the overall risk priority profile for each category of records and information

- *Step 9:* Identify system and control improvements and determine residual risk

Each step is discussed in detail in the following sections. Worked examples are provided to aid understanding.

Getting Started

The records and information risk assessment should start with decisions about how to define key concepts, the scope and focus of the risk assessment, and the approach to be used in conducting the assessment.

Clear definitions of key concepts are critical to the success of the risk assessment as they ensure that all stakeholders can communicate with and understand one another easily. They also ensure consistency of analysis over time. If the organization already has a corporate risk management strategy or program, definitions of key concepts may exist already. If not, they will have to be created. For example, before beginning to identify risks, risk managers will need to define the term "risk" if the organization does not have a definition used as part of a corporate risk management strategy or program. The glossary in Appendix B provides definitions of key risk management terminology. The additional readings in Appendix A will also be of help to individuals who need to create definitions.

Although the risk assessment exercise can be carried out on the entire organization as a one-time exercise or over time, other options are available. A more practical and useful approach may be to focus the risk assessment on one of the following:

- A division or business unit

- A particular business function or process (e.g., internal audit)

- A particular project

- A particular category of records

- Objectives and strategies

Decisions about the scope and focus of the risk assessment will result in different combinations of risk assessment analysis. For example:

- The records and information risks faced by a particular business unit

- The risks associated with a new project that has several functions
- An analysis of the risks presented by a particular category of records

Choice of the focus of analysis will be entirely dependent upon what is most appropriate to the organization's business context and risk assessment needs. The risk assessment framework is designed for flexibility of use.

Decisions also will have to be made about how to conduct the risk assessment and who should conduct it. A team or an individual may lead the risk assessment exercise. This team or individual may be part of a business unit responsible for risk management working in consultation with a records and information specialist(s) within the organization, or a records and information management team or specialist working in consultation with other business units. Although a specialist team or individual may lead the records and information risk assessment, it will not be effective unless senior management support the exercise. A mechanism also should exist to allow the team or individual leading the risk assessment to share findings with senior executives. This communication of findings might take the form of reporting to an executive level committee or an appropriate member of senior management such as a chief risk officer.

In addition, consideration must be given to strategies for gathering data for the risk assessment. A number of strategies can be used, for example:

- Consulting annual reports and other business documentation
- Conducting workshops or focus groups with relevant staff
- Conducting face-to-face interviews
- Working with a combination of these approaches

The approaches used in conducting the risk assessment and who conducts it depend upon and should be a good fit both with the organization's business context and culture and the scope and focus of the assessment. The following sections present ideas for how the assessment framework can be adapted to suit different business contexts, cultures, and areas of focus.

Creating worksheets for the risk assessment data using a spreadsheet software program may be useful. This software will enable automatic calculation of the quality level and risk profile and the overall risk priority profile for each category of records and information, and it will allow easy recalculation of risk data over time. A sample worksheet for the requirements-based approach is provided in Appendix C.

Key Learning Points

- Prepare clear definitions of key terms and concepts (e.g., risk) before starting the risk assessment.
- Identify the scope and focus of the risk assessment from the outset.
- Make decisions about how to and who will conduct the risk assessment before the risk assessment begins.
- Obtain senior management sponsorship and support – critical for success of the risk assessment.
- Use a spreadsheet-based worksheet for data collection and organization to facilitate automatic calculations and updates.

Step 1: Maintain the Strategic Picture

The requirements-based risk assessment methodology for records and information-related risks begins at the strategic level. (See Figure 7, page 50.) The strategic level is used to ensure that the data collected during the risk assessment is relevant to the objectives of the organization or the project under study. Maintaining a strategic picture during the risk assessment will help the organization identify and prioritize the risks that threaten achievement of strategic objectives.

An assessment linking records and information risks with the strategic picture will help risk managers identify how risks at the operational level, where the work gets done, have possible adverse impacts on the key business functions and strategic objectives of the organization. This approach is recommended highly to anyone wishing to use records and information risk management for more strategic purposes such as optimizing business opportunity. However, if management has no great concern with linking the results of the risk assessment to the strategic objectives of the organization, including this step is not essential to a records and information risk assessment exercise. If this step is excluded, step 8—calculation of the overall risk priority profile—also will be excluded from the assessment exercise.

To achieve the strategic picture, step 1 aims to identify and rank an organization's key business functions or its key strategies and objectives. If strategies and objectives are identified and ranked, they will need to be linked to the business functions that support their achievement. If the risk assessment is to focus on a particular business unit, the work performed by the business unit will need to be placed into the intellectual context of the organization's business functions or strategies and objectives to gain a sense of the unit's strategic importance to the organization as a whole. This type of analysis also will be the case if the assessment focuses on a particular project. At the same time, however, identifying and ranking the business unit's or project's particular functions or strategies and objectives may be useful.

Inevitably, ranking will be a subjective exercise. The importance of a particular function or strategic objective will depend on who is being asked. As much as possible, try to rank business functions or strategies and objectives in a manner that best reflects the current consensual perspective of the organization's board and/or senior management team. A consensual perspective may not be easy if disagreement exists among the board or senior management. In such a case, focusing on functions or strategies associated with the highest risk or those that are of particular concern at the moment and giving all other functions or strategic objectives a lower ranking may be helpful. Avoid ranking from the perspective of a single business unit or individual. Similarly, avoid relying solely on data drawn from other organizations or industry standards. These data may be helpful but, ideally, the rankings should reflect values appropriate to the organization being assessed.

The need to obtain a board or senior management perspective on business functions or strategies and objectives raises the question of how to gather this information. One approach is to have the issue raised at a board or senior management team meeting, though this tactic may be impractical if the organization is very large. Another approach may be to meet individually with board members or senior managers, gradually building up a picture of the organization's strategic priorities. If direct access to board members or senior managers is not possible, holding focus group meetings with a lower level of managers (e.g., operational or business process managers) can be useful, as senior managers should be communicating organizational priorities to this level. Alternatively, take an indirect approach by consulting

Key Learning Points

- Maintaining a strategic picture during the risk assessment ensures that data collection is linked to the organization's strategic objectives and makes the task of identifying and prioritizing the organization's risks easier.
- Step 1 entails identifying and ranking the organization's key business functions or its key strategies and objectives.
- Step 1 can be eliminated from the risk assessment exercise in organizations that are less concerned with using the results of the risk assessment for strategic management. If eliminated, step 8 of this methodology becomes redundant.

annual reports and other documents that discuss the organization's strategic objectives. Keep in mind that organizational priorities, and therefore their rankings, are likely to change at least annually.

Business functions or strategies and objectives ranked most important should be given a score of five, and those that are least important should receive a score of one. The same ranking can be given to more than one function or strategic objective. See Example 1.

Example 1: Identifying and Ranking Key Business Functions

Step 1: Identify and rank key business functions or strategies and objectives. The following table shows possible rankings for a hypothetical set of retail banking business functions.

Business Function	Ranking
Internal Audit	3
Branch Banking Operations	5
Commercial Credit	5
Financial Control	5
Treasury Management	5
Planning and Budgeting	4
Accounting and Analysis	4
Human Resources Analysis	3
General Services	2
Legal	3

Step 2: Focus on Business Processes

Business records and information are created and kept in transacting business processes that support business functions. Identifying and ranking business processes is an important part of identifying the records and information required to achieve an organization's strategic objectives and assess records and information-related risks. Along with step 1, identifying and ranking business processes helps to provide a strategic level picture. Identifying and ranking business processes, therefore, is recommended even when the scope and focus of the risk assessment is limited to a particular category of record.

Step 2 entails identifying and ranking the key business processes associated with a particular business function. This step can be carried out for all or a selected number of an organization's or project's business functions. Time and resource constraints on the assessment exercise may make identifying and ranking the business processes associated with only a single business function feasible. If so, the rankings assigned to each business function in step 1 can help to identify which business function(s) should take priority in the risk assessment.

If strategies and objectives were identified and ranked in step 1, before identifying and ranking the business processes, management needs to identify the business functions that help achieve those strategies and objectives. Once the business functions are identified, then the business processes that support those functions can be identified. If the focus of analysis is a particular project, a similar exercise is needed to identify the business functions linked to the project, followed by analysis of the business processes.

As in step 1, the relative importance of each business process should be ranked from one to five on the basis of how critical that process is to achieving the aims and objectives of the business function. Business processes ranked most important should be given a score of five; processes that are least important, a score of one.

Here again, ranking will be a subjective exercise. Business processes should be ranked in a manner that best reflects the current consensual perspective of the manager of the business function that the business processes support. If disagreement or difficulty in deciding on rankings occurs, focus on business processes associated with the highest risk or those processes that are of particular concern at the moment, and give all other processes a lower ranking.

The information to identify and rank business processes is best gathered from a meeting with the manager of the business function under which the business processes fall or a focus group meeting with business process managers. Gaining access to these managers will likely be easier than to senior managers. If the information for step 1 is to be obtained from an operational level of managers, data gathering for steps 1 and 2 may be combined. Relevant information also can be gathered from annual reports and documents that discuss the organization's strategic objectives and business functions and processes. Again, keep in mind that organizational priorities, and therefore their rankings, are likely to change at least annually. See Example 2.

Key Learning Points

- Along with step 1, identifying and ranking business processes helps maintain a strategic picture.
- Identifying and ranking the business processes is a necessary precursor to identifying and ranking records and information requirements because records and information are created and kept to support business processes.
- Step 2 entails identifying and ranking the business processes associated with a particular business function. It can be carried out for all business functions or only a select few.

Example 2: Identifying and Ranking Key Business Processes

Step 2: Identify and rank key business processes associated with all or a targeted business function. The following table shows possible rankings for the commercial credit area of the retail banking business processes:

Business Process	Ranking
Credit Policy Admin.	5
Credit Extension	5
Credit Servicing	4
Credit Collection	3

Step 3: Identify and Rank Records and Information Types and Requirements

Organizations such as the ones cited in Table 1, page 36, often experience problems when records and information:

- Do not meet the requirements needed to complete business transactions effectively

- Do not support internal and external accountabilities and controls over business transactions (e.g., internal audit or regulatory requirements designed to prevent process errors, conflicts of interest, etc.)

Though organizations require records to possess certain characteristics in order to support effective transaction processing and accountability, most often the identification of these requirements is not an explicit and conscious organizational exercise. Moreover, managers seldom explicitly and consciously identify the kinds of record-keeping systems that will be required to actually produce records and information of the necessary quality. Rather, they generally assume that such systems are in place or develop naturally. Oftentimes, these systems are not in place and do not develop, and, as a result, the organization's records creation and keeping practices fail to produce records of the quality needed to support organizational transaction processing and accountability systems, thereby exposing the organization to a range of risks. Consequently, ensuring that the organization's records and information support effective completion of business transactions and meet the requirements of internal and external accountabilities and controls is important. Step 3 is designed as a first step to ensuring that records are of the type to provide such support and meet necessary requirements.

Following identification of key business processes, the type and quality of records and information required to support these processes should be assessed. Time and resource constraints on the assessment exercise may make identifying and ranking the records and information types and requirements associated with only selected businesses processes feasible. If so, the rankings assigned to each business process in step 2 can help to identify which business processes should take priority in the risk assessment.

This assessment first must consider the types of records and information required under normal operating conditions to:

- Complete all transactions associated with the business process
- Support internal and external accountabilities and controls for those transactions effectively

Once the types of records have been identified, they should be ranked in order of importance from five for the most critical to one for the least critical. In undertaking the ranking, a strategy similar to that outlined in step 2 for ranking business processes may be used. In addition, retention schedules, where these exist, can also be useful indicators of the criticality of different records and information. Those records with longer retention periods and legal and regulatory requirements for retention generally tend to be more critical than records with shorter retention periods and no legal or regulatory requirement for retention. Similarly, if an organization has produced vital records schedules, these schedules can also be used as indicators of the criticality of different records and information.

When ranking records and information types, bear in mind that a form of documentation that is critical in the context of one business function may not be as critical in the context of another, particularly if the business function in question holds only a copy of the record or information. For example, an internal audit function may rely upon budget reports, budget worksheets, and expense invoices to conduct audits, but the audit department may not be the "office of record" for these types of documents. See Example 3.

Example 3: Ranking of the Importance of Record and Information Types

Step 3: Identify and rank the type of records and information required to complete business process transactions effectively and meet internal and external accountabilities. The following example is for the credit extension process:

Type of Record/Information	Criticality Ranking
Credit Files – Open	5
Credit Files – Closed	3
Daily Credit Extension Reports	3
Declined Credit Extension Applications	1
Credit Limit and Extension Policies	5

Next, identify the quality characteristics that the records and information must possess. Although the quality of records required will vary from organization to organization, important qualities to consider include:

- *Availability:* Are the necessary records and information being created? Are they available when needed?
- *Completeness:* Are the records complete, or is critical information missing?

- *Accuracy:* Are the records and information reliable? Are they kept up-to-date, or are they often outdated?

- *Authenticity:* Are the records and information created by a reliable source? Are they validated? Are they kept secure from alteration and tampering?

- *Timely accessibility:* What are the general time frames in which the records are required under normal conditions? Under extraordinary conditions? Are the records available within these time frames?

- *Relevance:* Are existing records and information relevant enough?

- *Comparability:* How comparable do the records and information have to be to other records and information? Over time?

The list of records qualities in Table 3, page 47, provides additional examples to consider in regard to the characteristics that records and information may need to have in order to support completion of business transactions and meet the requirements of internal and external accountabilities. Additionally, very often laws and regulations specify the types and attributes of records and information that must be created for specific business processes.

A decision may have been made to focus the risk assessment on a particular category of record or system. If the assessment is specific, step 3 will entail assessing the quality characteristics required to support completion and meet internal and external accountabilities and controls for transactions of only one type of record or a particular system. The quality characteristics of a given record type or system can be assessed effectively only with reference to the requirements of the business process to which the records or systems relate, however.

The following example of tracking bad debts is illustrative of the analytical process involved in step 3. For the purposes of effective financial management, managers of a business enterprise may want to track their bad debts. In order to do so, they will need to communicate reliably how the organization defines a bad debt and the level of such debt that is acceptable. They also will rely on subordinates to pull together reports on the status of customer accounts in relation to their definition of bad debt. In order to meet management's internal control and decision-making needs, the bad debt reports will need to possess certain characteristics. For instance, the reliability of the reports may be determined by the extent of comprehensiveness, accuracy, and completeness in depicting the status of customer accounts in relation to organizational definitions of what constitutes bad debt. As much as possible, these quality characteristics should be quantified. For example, management may decide that reports must be 99 percent accurate, etc. Bad debt reports also may need to present information in a form that permits comparisons over time so that managers can determine whether the number of bad debts is increasing or decreasing in relation to organizational limits and past experience. Depending on the level of risk, managers also may need these reports to reflect daily, weekly, monthly, or quarterly bad debt positions—that is, whatever time frame permits them to take action to correct deviations from acceptable levels of bad debt quickly enough to avoid operating problems. From this analysis, management should be able to identify and quantify the quality characteristics required of records and information supporting the business transaction, for example, reliability, completeness, accuracy, comparability, and timeliness.

The bad debts example shows how the type of records required will vary according to the type of business activity in which the organization is engaged and the particular manner in which it conducts its business. Because of these variations, directors and managers of organizations can rely only to an extent on industry guidelines or standards to determine their information requirements. Overreliance on industry standards may cause managers to overlook important requirements that are specific to their particular enterprise.

A number of methods are available for gathering data for this step. Managers doing the risk assessment may want to consider conducting some initial research into the records and information requirements of chosen business processes. Often, this sort of information may be available from records classification manuals, retention schedules, computer system requirements documentation, workflow analysis, or knowledge asset inventories. This initial research may be followed by one-to-one interviews or a focus group meeting with relevant managers and employees. Try to make this process as intuitive as possible for the business process owners by appealing to their understanding and knowledge of the work they perform. See Example 4.

Example 4: **Identifying the Types and Quality Requirements of Records and Information**

Step 3: Identify the type and quality of records and information required to complete business process transactions effectively and to meet internal and external accountabilities. The following list contains possible types of information needed to meet the information requirements of the credit extension business process. Note that the bulk of this information should be found in the credit file.

- Details of each transaction, including the parties to the loan, advance, or other credit exposure (Note: Ensure that the parties are identified because failure to do so may affect the ability to recover on a non-performing asset. Also, obtain full name, address, and contact information for all borrowers, which must be kept up-to-date.).

- Determine whether and, if so, who is subparticipated, the amount and currency
  - The contract, rollover, value, and settlement or repayment dates
  - The contractual interest rates of an interest rate transaction or commitment
  - The contractual exchange rate for a foreign exchange transaction or commitment
  - The contractual commission or fee payable or receivable together with any other related payment or receipt
  - The nature and current estimated value of any security for a loan or other exposure
  - The physical location and documentary evidence of such security
  - The nature and book value of any asset upon which the loan or other credit exposure is secured
  - Information about margins of securities accepted for collateral as a ratio of asset value to value of security; all securities documentation must be 100 percent accurate

---

- Information indicating the full extent of credit facilities extended to each individual client and the status of those facilities

---

- Information relating to the full extent of credit guaranteed by a single individual

- Details of any off-balance sheet asset origination, sale, and servicing of various types of credit, including contractual fee arrangements

- Details of credit limits authorized by management that are appropriate to the type, nature, and volume of the business undertaken; where relevant, the limits should include counterparty, industry sector, country, settlement, liquidity, interest rate mismatch, and securities position limits

- Information concerning the factors considered, the analysis undertaken, and the approval or rejection by management of a loan or other credit facility

- On a memorandum basis, details of every transaction entered into in the name of and on behalf of another party on an agency or fiduciary basis where the bank is not legally or contractually bound by the transaction

- Reports to management on the number, type, industry, counterparty, amount, and other details of credit facilities granted to track various risks

Once records and information requirements are identified, ranking them is useful. Improving records and information management systems and controls to prevent or mitigate risks can be an expensive undertaking. Ranking records and information requirements will help to set priorities in determining which weaknesses in records and information management systems and controls to address first. This decision will help to ensure that resources are used wisely.

To carry out this step, rank the relative importance of the identified quality characteristics for each type of information or record, from five for most important to one for least important. The data for this step can be gathered in a manner similar to the previous step and may even be collected at the same time.

As with earlier steps, ranking will be a subjective exercise. Quality characteristics should be ranked in a manner that best reflects the current consensual perspective of the owners of the business process. If disagreement or difficulty in deciding on rankings exists, focus on those quality characteristics associated with the highest risk or those characteristics that are of particular concern at the moment, and give all other qualities a lower ranking. See Example 5.

Key Learning Points

- Identification of records and information requirements, and the systems needed to meet these requirements, often is not a conscious and systematic organizational activity, which can give rise to records and information-related risks.
- Step 3 entails identifying and ranking the type and quality of records and information needed to support business processes and related internal and external accountabilities. Step 3 can be carried out for all business processes or a select few.
- Records classification manuals, records retention schedules, vital records schedules, computer system requirements documentation, knowledge asset inventories, workflow analysis, and laws and regulations can provide useful data on records and information requirements.

Example 5: Ranking Quality Characteristics

Step 3: For each category of record and information, rank the quality characteristics required to complete business process transactions effectively and meet internal and external accountabilities. The following table contains possible quality characteristics and rankings for open credit files.

Quality	Ranking of Quality Importance
Created/Availability	5
Completeness	5
Accuracy	5
Authenticity	5
Accessibility	4
Comparability	2

Step 4: Conduct Systems and Controls Gap Analysis

Records and information systems and controls exist to prevent or mitigate risks that can arise when quality characteristics are not met. Evaluating the gap between ideal quality requirements and the degree to which existing systems and controls meet those requirements helps an organization determine where weaknesses in systems and controls may introduce risk from operating or other problems. Figure 8 illustrates the process.

Records and information systems and controls permeate the entire organization, at all levels and in all functions. They include a range of possible actions that should fit the organization's needs and be influenced by the way the organization is structured and managed and by the type and complexity of its transactions and commitments. Effectiveness of these controls is assessed in step 4. Though specific systems and controls must match organizational requirements, the following systems and controls can be singled out for special attention:

- Organizational recordkeeping structure and lines of authority
- Procedural rules (e.g., over the destruction of records to ensure that unauthorized destructions do not take place or over the way in which records are accessed)

Systems and Controls Gap Analysis

Figure 8

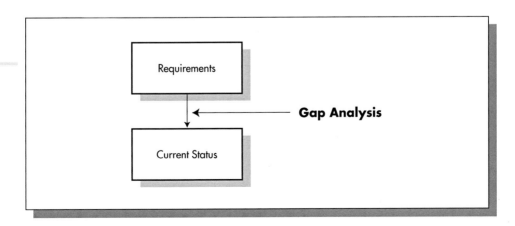

- Segregation of duties (e.g., between employees responsible for designing a system, maintaining it, and transacting business)
- Authorization and approval (e.g., appropriate authorization and approvals for records creation and destruction)
- Personnel (e.g., qualified staff performing appropriate functions and with appropriate training to perform records control activities and understand the importance of these controls)
- Levels and effectiveness of system integration

The analytical process in this step involves identifying the degree to which each quality characteristic for a particular type of record or information is satisfied by existing records and information systems and controls. Information that a study of current information systems and controls may reveal include:

- Existing controls need improving
- Existing controls need to be replaced
- Controls are absent

Those quality characteristics that are fully satisfied by existing systems and controls should receive a ranking of five, while those characteristics least satisfied should receive a ranking of one.

To gather the data needed to complete step 4, individuals conducting the assessment may want to carry out some initial research into the records and information systems and controls for each category of record or information needed to support a particular business process or the particular type of record that is the focus of the assessment. Knowledge held by an organization's records and information specialist(s) will be useful during this process. These individuals will know about and understand existing records and information systems and controls.

Initial research likely will need to be supplemented by one-to-one interviews or a focus group meeting with business process managers and employees. Because the analytic work is fairly intensive and may lead to overload, avoid combining data gathering for step 4 with data gathering for step 3.

Time also can be taken at this stage to analyze the underlying reasons that existing records and information systems and controls do not satisfy quality characteristics, if they do not. This type of analysis may be approached in many ways. Some commonly recommended techniques for conducting this analysis include:

- Cause-and-effect diagrams (sometimes referred to as "fishbone" diagrams)—graphical representations of the causes of various events (e.g., structures, people, controls, and technology)
- Analysis of blockages in critical success factors. For example, ask business process owners to identify difficulties they are currently experiencing in obtaining the quality of records and information they require to perform their work or meet internal and external accountabilities. Often, in the course of discussing such difficulties, the

Key Learning Points

- Evaluating the gap between records and information requirements and the degree to which existing systems and controls meet these requirements helps an organization determine where weaknesses in systems and controls may introduce risks.
- Step 4 entails analyzing the degree to which each record and information quality requirement for a particular type of record is satisfied by existing records and information systems and controls.
- Analysis of the underlying causes of systems and controls weaknesses may also be carried out at this point in the risk assessment.

causes of weaknesses in records and information systems and controls will become apparent.

- Decision trees—graphical representations of possible events resulting from various decisions
- Six Sigma™ methodology[78]
- Workflow analysis[79]

Results of the analysis should be recorded for future reference. See Example 6. More information about these and other methodologies for identifying root causes of weaknesses in records and information controls can be found in the further readings listed in Appendix A.[80]

Example 6: Ranking the Level of Satisfaction with Importance of Quality Requirements

Step 4: Identify the degree to which current records and information management systems and controls satisfy each quality requirement. The following table contains possible quality characteristics and rankings for quality and level of satisfaction for open credit files:

Quality	Ranking of Quality Importance	Ranking of Level of Satisfaction
Created/Availability	5	4
Completeness	5	3
Accuracy	5	3
Authenticity	5	4
Accessibility	4	3
Comparability	2	4

Step 5: Calculate the Effectiveness Rating

A records and information systems and controls effectiveness rating may be calculated from the rankings given in steps 3 and 4. This rating is useful as a means of high-

---

[78] Six Sigma™ is a methodology that uses data and statistical analysis to measure and improve an organization's operational performance by identifying and eliminating defects in manufacturing and services. More information about this methodology is available at www.isixsigma.com/library/content/six-sigma-newbie.asp, accessed 08 March 2004.

[79] David Loader, in *Controls, Procedures and Risks*, 39, 51–52, and 67–70, provides helpful ideas on how to identify root causes of risks using workflow analysis.

[80] See, in particular, UK Office of Government Commerce, *Management of Risk*, Annex H: Information on Further Techniques to Support Management of Risk.

lighting and prioritizing the need to address weaknesses in existing systems, as well as calculating the risk profiles in steps 7 and 8.

To calculate the effectiveness rating for a given type of record or information, follow the formula presented in Figure 9.

**Effectiveness
Rating Formula**

Figure 9

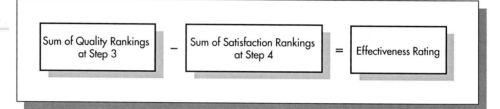

The resulting rating is counter-intuitive in the sense that the higher the resulting number, the lower the level of effectiveness. The effectiveness rating is designed to work with the risk calculations in steps 7 and 8 because a low level of effectiveness of existing records and information systems and controls increases the level of risk. See Example 7.

Example 7: **Calculating the Effectiveness Rating**

Step 5: Calculate the records and information systems and controls effectiveness rating.

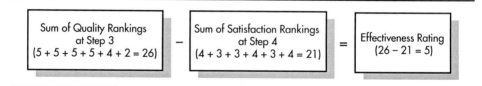

Key Learning Points

- The effectiveness rating provides a numeric indicator of the degree of weakness in existing systems and controls for a particular record or information type.
- This rating can be used to help set priorities for the treatment of records and information systems and controls weaknesses.
- A high effectiveness rating indicates a higher level of risk.
- Calculation of the effectiveness rating is needed in order to complete the calculations at steps 7 and 8 of the records and information risk assessment methodology.

Step 6: Perform Risk Identification and Assessment

Risk identification and assessment is the core of the requirements-based risk assessment methodology. However, it cannot be carried out without first undertaking the analysis outlined in steps 3 to 5. This particular risk assessment methodology—requirements-based risk assessment—emphasizes identifying the risks to the organization if records and information required for transacting and controlling business processes are not available or of the desired quality.

As mentioned previously, this approach differs from most other existing approaches to identifying and managing records and information risks. Existing approaches tend to focus on threats to an organization's records and information arising from disasters, computer failures, or security breaches. The traditional approach emphasizes the risk to records from given threats. By identifying the risks to the organization if required records and information are not available or of the desired quality, the central focus of this risk assessment methodology is on the risks to the organization's strategic business objectives from weaknesses in records and information. The causes of these weaknesses may come from any number of sources, including, but by no means limited to, disasters, computer failures, or security breaches. The advantage of using this approach is that the strategic focus is never lost because the relationship is made explicit between records and information and achievement of an organization's strategies and objectives. By using this approach, the impact of records and information risks on the organization is easier to see and to justify changes to records and information systems and controls to prevent or mitigate these risks. The requirements-based risk assessment approach is also more effective in identifying systemic types of records and information risk.

Step 6 entails four important activities:

1. Identifying risks to the business
2. Identifying the causes of those risks

Tip

Thinking about these risks in the context of the organization's system of risk classification may be helpful. If the organization does not have an enterprise-wide taxonomy of risks, referring to the classification schemes presented on pages 13–15 may be helpful.

3. Ranking risks according to likelihood of occurrence
4. Identifying the consequences of risks and ranking them according to their severity

Figure 10 illustrates the process to be followed.

Step 4 will have provided information about the risks to the availability or the quality of the organization's records and information arising from current systems and controls. To identify the risks to the business from identified risks to, or weaknesses of, records and information, data gathering should be geared to capturing as many of the key risks as possible within the time allotted for the risk assessment exercise. Capturing

Risk Identification and Assessment

Figure 10

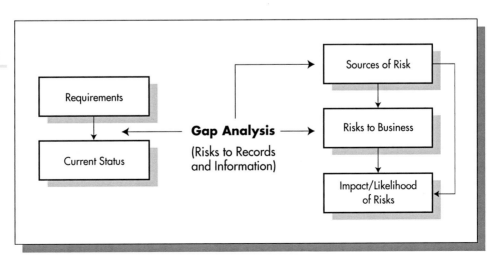

Tip

Remember to look at risk proximity when assessing risk probability or likelihood; that is, whether the risk is likely to occur within a given time frame and how often within that time frame the risk is likely to occur. When assessing the impact or consequences of a risk, remember to look at both direct and indirect costs, as well as the scope and number of occurrences of the impact.

information about any dependencies between these risks at this point is also important, as a risk in one area of the organization may trigger other risks.

Identification of causes, or sources, of risk follows identification of risks. Some or all this data may have been gathered during step 4. If not, gather it now.

The next activity consists of identifying the impact or consequences of risks and ranking them according to their severity. A risk can have one or more consequences or impacts. Each consequence or impact will have some measurable cost to the organization, which should be identified as far as possible. For example, the financial cost of loss of accounts payable information because of a fire caused by an electrical fault might be calculated by assessing financial losses as a result of being unable to take advantage of prompt payment schemes negotiated with vendors. Each risk should be given a ranking from one to five based on the perceived consequences to the area or to the organization as a whole, with one being the least consequential (e.g., minor loss), and five being the most (e.g., devastating loss with extremely high impact).

Using a predefined classification scheme may be helpful when assessing areas of possible impact upon the business. For example, management may want to consider the following types of risk and possible consequences or impacts:

- Strategic risk: Would loss, damage, or unrecoverability of the records and information threaten the organization's strategic position?

- Financial risk: Would loss, damage, or unrecoverability of the records and information result in financial losses or threaten the organization's financial position?

- Legal risk: Would loss, damage, or unrecoverability of the records and information result in litigation or noncompliance with laws or regulations?

- Reputational risk: Would loss, damage, or unrecoverability of the records and information result in damage to the organization's public image, confidence, or reputation?

- Operational risk: Would loss, damage, or unrecoverability of the records and information prevent the organization from completing business transactions effectively?

Next, each risk should be ranked according to the probability or likelihood of its occurrence. For example, if loss of accounts payable information because of a fire caused by an electrical fault is one of the identified risks, individuals doing the risk assessment might indicate that the risk has a 1 percent chance of occurring. Assessing the likelihood of a risk will be dependent on the understanding of the underlying causes of the risked event. Rank the probability of each risk from one to five, with five being for the most likely to occur, and one for the least likely.

Necessary data can be gathered in a number of ways. Risk managers may consult relevant documents to gather data, conduct one-to-one interviews, or hold a series of focus group meetings. The exact approach should fit well with the business context of

Key Learning Points

- The core of the risk assessment exercise is the iden-tification and assessment of risks to the organiza-tion's strategic business objectives from weaknesses in records and information.
- Step 6 entails the following four important activities:
  1. Identifying risks to the business
  2. Identifying the causes of those risks
  3. Ranking risks according to likelihood of occur-rence
  4. Identifying the consequences of risks and rank-ing them according to their severity
- Data that reveal patterns of past occurrence or managers' opinions about the likely probability and impact will help in the assessment of the probability and impact of risks.

the organization, the organization's culture, and the time and resources available for conducting the risk assessment. Gather data about the pattern of past occurrences of risks and their impact, or collect managers' opinions about the likely proba-bility and impact of risks. See Example 8.

Example 8: Identifying and Ranking Types of Risks by Likelihood and Consequence

Step 6: Identify and rank (by likelihood and con-sequence) the types of risks to the organization from gaps between quality requirements and the quality of records and information delivered by existing systems and controls. The following table shows possible types of risk and the ranking of those risks for each quality characteristic:

Quality	Type of Risk	Ranking of Consequence	Ranking of Probability
Created/ Availability	Potential for legal risk because a loan is effectively nonexistent if it is not documented. Credit risk is also possible because a loan cannot be tracked or monitored.	5	1
Completeness	Legal and credit risk again are possible if documen-tation is not complete; e.g., it can lead to uncertainty about the parties to a loan, the terms of the loan, and an inability to track or monitor the loan.	5	3
Accuracy	Same as above.	5	3
Authenticity	Documents may be altered after the fact and may not be suitable as evidence in a legal dispute.	4	1
Accessibility	If a loan file cannot be found, the parties to, terms, and status of the loan cannot be determined, which can result in loss because of legal and credit risk; slow retrieval will also affect customer service.	5	4
Comparability	Quality issues can lead to uncertainty about the quality of the loan and its legal status.	3	1

Step 7: Calculate Quality Level and Risk Profiles

At this stage of the risk assessment, managers should have a clear idea of the records and information requirements for each type of record or information needed to support business processes and functions and of the risks to the organization if these requirements are not met. The purpose of step 7 is to express these findings in numeric terms; that is, as a calculation to arrive at a quality level and risk profile for each type of record or information.

The resulting number will have no inherent significance (i.e., it is qualitative), but it does serve to indicate relative levels of quality and risk when compared across record types or over time for a single record type. Thus, working out the quality level and risk profile for a single record type will be meaningful only if the intention is to compare values over time or with values for other record types. This step can be omitted if managers have no desire to make these comparisons. Such comparisons can be helpful, however, if they are used to set priorities for improving records and information systems and controls within the organization or to measure improvements over time.

Use the quality level and risk profile formula presented in Figure 11 to calculate the quality level and risk profile for a record type. See Example 9.

Quality Level and Risk Profile Formula

Figure 11

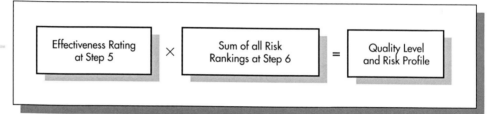

Example 9: Calculating the Quality Level and Risk Profile

Step 8: Calculate the quality level and risk profile for each category of record and information.

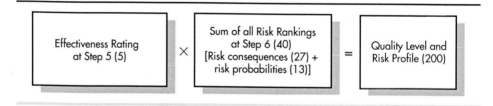

![key icon] **Key Learning Points**

- The quality level and risk profile is a numeric expression of the degree to which records and information requirements are met for specific record and information types.
- Though the number has no inherent significance, its usefulness lies in its ability to help in making comparisons among record and information types or over time for a single record and information type. This step can be eliminated if managers have no desire to make such comparisons.

Step 8: Calculate the Overall Priority Profile

Before making changes to records and information systems and controls to address weaknesses in the availability and quality of records needed to reduce risk, evaluate which systems and controls will be most useful if improved. Generally speaking, these systems and controls will be records and information systems and controls for which:

- The overall importance of the business function and process with which the record is associated is high.
- The overall importance of the record and information type is high.
- The overall importance of the desired record and information quality is high.
- The level of satisfaction with the current quality of the records and information in relation to required quality is low.
- The effectiveness of current records and information systems and controls is low.
- The risk to the organization associated with failures to meet records and information quality requirements is high, both in terms of probability and impact.

The overall priority profile for each record type is a score designed to indicate the record category and for which of its required qualities it will be of the greatest strategic importance, using the above criteria, to ensure that adequate records and information systems and controls are in place.

As in step 7, the resulting number will have no inherent significance, but it will indicate relative levels of risk when compared across record types or over time for a single record type. Like the quality level and risk profile, the overall priority profile can be helpful in determining priorities for action to improve records and information systems and controls. Because making such improvements can be costly, having an indicator of which areas would be most beneficial to address first can often be helpful.

Calculation of the overall priority profile will be possible only if steps 1 and 2 have been performed. Step 8 involves multiplying the ranking for the business function to which the records and information type relates (assigned at step 1), times the ranking for the business process to which the records and information type relates (assigned at step 2), times the ranking of the records and information type (assigned at step 3), times the quality level and risk profile score determined for each record in step 7.

Use the formula in Figure 12 to calculate the overall priority profile for a record type. See Example 10.

Overall Priority Profile Formula

Figure 12

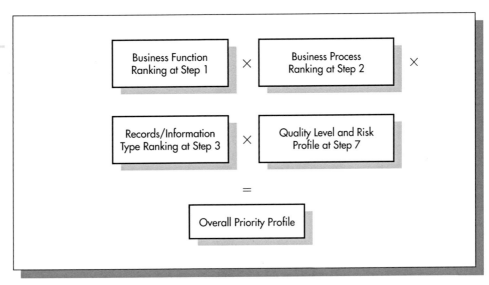

Example 10: Calculating the Overall Risk Priority Profile

Step 8: Calculate the overall risk priority profile for each category of record and information.

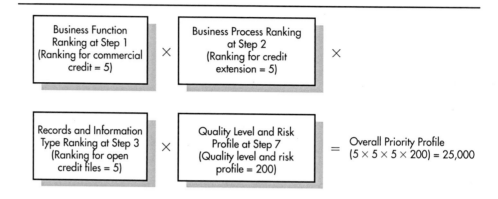

Key Learning Points

- The overall priority profile is a numeric indicator of the records and information type, and those of its requirements, for which it will be of the most strategic importance to address weaknesses in systems and controls.
- Though the number has no inherent significance, its usefulness lies in its ability to help in making comparisons among records and information types and over time for a single record and information type.
- Calculation of the overall priority profile is possible only if steps 1 and 2 have been completed.

Step 9: Use the Assessment Results

No risk assessment is carried out as an intellectual exercise. Its effectiveness must be measured, first and foremost, by the results it achieves in reducing or mitigating the effects of risks. Thus, once priorities for records and information systems and controls improvements have been identified, the types of changes needed to deliver the required quality of records and information, and thereby reduce the level of risk, must be identified as part of the corporate risk management strategy and regularly monitored. As operational risk expert David Loader observes, "Controls are crucially important and . . . managers need to take time to analyze the type of control that is truly suited to a process. Then they need to decide how the control should be monitored and managed and finally they need to know how effective the control is."[81]

Changes to systems and controls need not be designed to eliminate risks entirely. In fact, totally eliminating risks is likely to prove impossible. Rather, the focus should be on bringing risks down to acceptable and manageable levels according to the organization's risk tolerance level.

As discussed in Part One, managers can pursue a number of different risk mitigation strategies. For example, by introducing a regular electrical maintenance program, the likelihood of fire because of an electrical problem can be reduced. Alternatively, the

[81] David Loader, *Controls, Procedures and Risk*, 66.

impact of the risk event could be reduced by producing backup copies or duplicates of critical records and information, as is standard practice in business continuity programs. The earlier analysis carried out as part of steps 4 and 6 will provide the data necessary to identify appropriate changes or even additions to systems and controls.

Note that, as in the previous example, changes needed to reduce risk and ensure the required quality of records and information may not involve improving or changing a records and information system or control. It may mean making a change to some other system or control (e.g., a building maintenance program). This type of change underscores the importance of senior management support and overall organizational coordination of risk management. Effective management of records and information-related risks is likely to involve cooperation between various corporate functions and organizational units. Therefore, risk mitigation strategies are best carried out in a holistic and systematic way as part of an enterprise-wide risk management program.

Although the primary goal of the records and information risk assessment should be to reduce organizational risk, the data gathered during the risk assessment exercise also can be used to enhance the strategic effectiveness of the organization's records and information management program. For example, the effectiveness of existing records and information systems and controls can be benchmarked with the effectiveness rating at step 5 and used to evaluate program effectiveness over time. The results of the assessment exercise also may help in developing operating plans for an organization's records and information management program by highlighting areas where improvements to existing records and information systems and controls will have the greatest strategic effect.

Control and monitoring of the implementation of new or enhanced systems and controls are critical to the success of effectively managing risk. This control includes assigning ownership of all risk treatment strategies to a sponsoring manager and identifying timelines in which implementation of changes to systems and controls will be completed and their effectiveness reviewed.

Measurements of effectiveness for risk treatment strategies should be agreed in advance and be SMART—specific, measurable, achievable, realistic, and timely. Key risk indicators and metrics (e.g., the number of late deliveries, rejected parts, or staff turnover) are examples of SMART measures of risk treatment strategies that managers can use to assess effectiveness.

Ongoing monitoring of the effectiveness of risk treatment strategies is important because new developments and changes in the organization and its business environment are inevitable. These changes may make developing new or altering existing systems and controls designed to manage identified risks a necessity. In particular, risk treatment strategies may become outdated when the following changes occur:

- Strategic priorities change.
- New organizational functions are added.
- Environmental changes occur (e.g., new threats arise or new laws or regulations are adopted).

- Records requirements change because of changes in the organization's culture or because of evolving business needs.

The process and procedures for tracking and monitoring implementation and effectiveness of risk treatment strategies should be set once appropriate changes and/or additions to systems and controls have been determined, ownership for risk treatments has been assigned, and timelines for implementation and review worked out. Consider how reporting on implementation and effectiveness of the risk treatment strategy will be achieved; how the reports will be used, when, and by whom; and how to ensure commitment to the quality of reporting. The risk register is a basic control tool managers can use to carry out this work.

Conducting a records and information risk assessment, such as outlined in this methodology, is often a time-consuming and resource-intensive undertaking. The potential benefits to the organization, however, in terms of managed risks, improved strategic effectiveness, and improved effectiveness of an organization's records and information program, make the effort highly worthwhile.

Key Learning Points

- Reducing or mitigating the effects of risks is the goal of the risk assessment exercise, though it can also be used to enhance the effectiveness of the organization's records and information management program.
- Making use of the risk assessment exercise entails determining what changes/additions to systems and controls are needed to manage risks effectively, monitoring implementation of these changes/additions, and evaluating their effectiveness.
- Changes needed to address records and information weaknesses may not necessarily involve making changes to records and information systems and controls; rather, changes to other systems and controls may be needed (e.g., building maintenance).
- Effective risk management requires senior-level management support and is best carried out as part of an enterprise-wide risk management program.

Adapting the Risk Assessment Methodology to an Event-Based Approach

As previously discussed, organizations traditionally have identified and managed their records and information risks by type of trigger event or threat—for example, the threat to records and information arising from disasters or security breaches. These threats are commonly addressed in the context of such programs as business continuity planning, IT security, and the like. As the event-based approach has been the more commonly used approach to identifying and dealing with records and information risks, many more tools and methods have been created to support this mode of analysis than exist to support a records and information requirements-based approach.[82] *Managing Risk for Records and Information*, therefore, focuses more on presenting a methodology for assessing risks arising from shortfalls in meeting records and information requirements. Nevertheless, understanding how

[82] See, for example, Jones and Keyes, *Emergency Management for Records and Information Management Programs*.

the records and information-based risk assessment methodology can be adapted to suit an event-based approach to assessing records and information-related risks still is useful for giving managers the option of using this approach when appropriate.

The adapted event-based methodology consists of the following nine steps:

- *Step 1:* Identify and rank key business functions or strategies and objectives.
- *Step 2:* Identify and rank key business processes associated with all or a targeted business function.
- *Step 3:* Identify and rank the type of records and information required to complete business process transactions effectively and meet internal and external accountabilities.
- *Step 4:* Identify possible risk trigger events or threats for each type of record and information.
- *Step 5:* Assess the effectiveness of current controls.
- *Step 6:* Identify the probability that identified trigger events/threats will occur and their impact on the business.
- *Step 7:* Calculate the risk profile for the type of record and information.
- *Step 8:* Calculate the overall risk priority profile for each type of record and information.
- *Step 9:* Identify systems and controls improvements.

The main difference between the requirements-based methodology and the event-based adaptation is that an analysis of a particular business function's records and information quality requirements is not necessary. Rather, simply identify what types of records and information are needed to complete the function's business transactions and then analyze the possible threats to the required records and information. Completing an event-based risk assessment can take less time and fewer resources. However, managers will miss out on gaining a comprehensive understanding of the organization's records and information requirements and the systematic types of risks to which a failure to meet these requirements can give rise.

Key Learning Points

- Many more tools and methodologies are available to support an event-based approach to records and information risk assessment than to support a requirements-based approach because the event-based approach is more common.
- The main difference between the requirements-based methodology and the event-based adaptation is that the adaptation does not require managers to analyze the records and information requirements of the organization's business functions.

The following sections present a nine-step adaptation of the requirements-based methodology presented in previous sections for use in conducting event-based records and information risk assessments. See Figure 13. The main focus of the discussion is on comparing and contrasting the adapted event-based methodology with the requirements-based methodology. Worked examples are provided to aid understanding where the steps differ from the requirements-based approach. Where the activities are not significantly different, readers should refer to the appropriate sections of the requirements-based methodology for full details on how to conduct each step.

Event-Based
Risk Assessment
Methodology

Figure 13

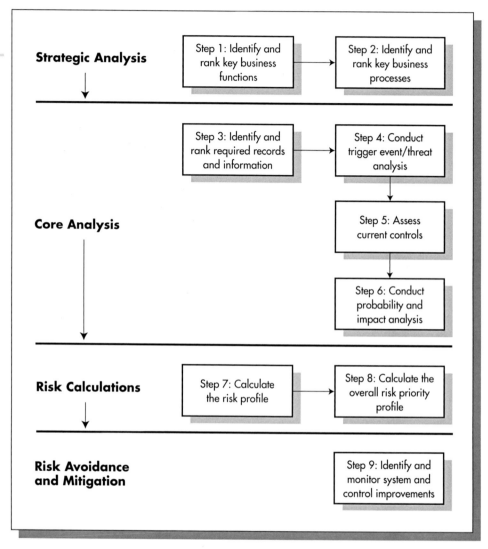

Getting Started

Just as with the requirements approach, effective event-based records and information risk assessment depends upon clearly defining the terms and concepts to use for the analysis. Create definitions if they do not exist already.

Define the scope and focus of the assessment exercise. Perhaps focus on a particular part of the business, a project, or a specific trigger event or threat.

As with the requirements-based methodology, managers will need to make decisions and plan for how data will be gathered and who will gather it. Here again, a worksheet can be a helpful tool to ensure that data gathering is consistent and complete. A sample worksheet for the event-based approach to using the records and information risk assessment methodology is included in Appendix D.

Steps 1 and 2: Conduct Strategic Analysis

As with the requirements-based methodology, steps 1 and 2 of the adapted event-based methodology are optional. They will, however, help identify the high-priority functions and processes of the organization in order to concentrate the risk assessment and control activities on critical areas.

Methods for conducting the strategic analysis is also the same for the requirements-based methodology and the adapted event-based methodology: Managers can use the methods outlined in steps 1 and 2 of the requirements-based risk assessment methodology for ranking business functions and processes (see pages 52-56).

Remember that if either of these steps is eliminated, performing the calculation at step 8 will not be possible.

Key Learning Points

- Steps 1 and 2 are designed to help managers identify the high-priority functions and processes of their organization in order to concentrate the risk assessment on critical areas.
- The same procedures should be followed for steps 1 and 2 of the event-based adaptation as for steps 1 and 2 of the requirements-based methodology.
- Steps 1 and 2 are optional, but if eliminated, they will prevent completion of the calculations at step 8.

Step 3: Identify and Rank Required Records and Information

This step entails identifying the type of records and information required to complete business process transactions effectively and meet internal and external accountabilities. However, if the focus is on the risk assessment of a particular type of record or information (e.g., a category of vital record), step 3 will not be necessary. If not, follow the methodology outlined in step 3 of the requirements-based methodology (see pages 56–61). Identification of the quality characteristics that the required records and information need to possess also will not be needed.

After the required records and information have been identified, rank them from one to five—five being the most critical and one being the least—to assist in setting priorities for the remainder of the risk assessment exercise. Once again, this step will, of course, not be necessary if a particular category of record or information is to be analyzed. See Example 11.

Example 11: Event-Based Methodology—Identifying and Ranking Types of Records and Information

Step 3: Identify and rank the type of records and information required to complete business process transactions effectively and meet internal and external accountabilities. The following example is for an internal audit function:

Type of Record/ Information	Criticality Ranking
Annual audit (signed)	5
Audit work papers	5
Audit copy of debits and credits to loans and discounts	1
Budget reports	3
Budget worksheets	1
Expense invoices	1

Key Learning Points

- Step 3 entails identifying the type of records and information required to complete business processes and meet internal and external accountabilities.
- Unlike the requirements-based methodology, the event-based adaptation does not require identification and analysis of records and information quality characteristics.
- Step 3 is not necessary if the risk assessment is focused on a particular record type.

Step 4: Conduct Trigger Event/Threat Analysis

The identification of a complete range of trigger events or threats that present risks to the target records and information is essential only if managers wish to avoid, transfer, or reduce the likelihood of that event or threat. If the plan is to focus risk treatment strategies only on reducing the impact of any given risk event once it occurs—as in the case of many business continuity initiatives—identifying all sources of the risk will not be essential. Simply assess the likely impact upon the business if the risk event does occur so that the organization can take steps to bring the business impact in line with the organization's risk tolerance levels. Although having a clear idea of the trigger events that can give rise to the risk probably will help in assessing risk impact, it can still be done with only a general idea of the most likely types of trigger events or threats.

To identify a wide range of possible trigger events or threats, begin by surveying the organization's business environment. The examples of typical trigger events and threats listed in Table 2, page 45, may provide some ideas to assist in getting started. Brainstorming sessions, SWOT analysis (identifying strengths, weaknesses, opportunities, and threats), and similar techniques as outlined in Part One can also be useful. After identifying a number of different trigger events or threats, management may decide to concentrate on only one or two that seem riskier or more threatening. Conducting an on-site survey of the organization's facilities and storage areas also can provide valuable information about potential threats. Look for such problem areas as leaky roofs, fire hazards, the absence of fire-suppression equipment, and insect infestation, for example.[83]

Key Learning Points

- Step 4 entails identifying a range of trigger events or threats to required records and information.
- Step 4 is necessary only if the objective is to avoid, transfer, or reduce the likelihood of a trigger event or threat but not if the objective is only to reduce its impact once it has occurred.
- Techniques, such as a SWOT analysis and others listed in Part One, or site surveys may be used to identify potential trigger events or threats.

---

[83] Jones and Keyes, *Emergency Management for Records and Information Management Programs*, 30.

Step 5: Assess Current Controls

A risk assessment that focuses on trigger events or threats should assess the effectiveness of any controls currently in place to mitigate the risk event. Undertaking this step is an important precursor to assessing the impact of the trigger event or threat (step 6) and will help identify additional measures and improvements that may be necessary to further mitigate the risk (step 9).

One of the best ways of assessing the effectiveness of current controls is to conduct a worst-case scenario analysis. Develop a scenario of what would happen if the threat materializes, given the existing state of current systems and controls. Are these systems and controls sufficient to control the risk to acceptable levels of tolerance? If not, this information should be reflected in the impact ranking assigned at step 6.

Key Learning Points

- Step 5 entails assessing the effectiveness of current systems and controls in guarding against or mitigating the effects of potential threats to required records and information.
- Step 5 is an important precursor to assessing the impact of the trigger event or threat (step 6) and will help managers identify additional measures and improvements that may be necessary to further mitigate the risk (step 9).
- A worst-case scenario analysis can help managers assess the effectiveness of current systems and controls.

Step 6: Conduct Probability and Impact Analysis

Next, identify the risks to the business if a particular trigger event or threat materializes, its likelihood of occurring, and the effects on the organization's operations if it does occur, given the state of existing systems and controls. Figure 14 shows the flow of the analysis.

Event-Based
Probability and
Impact Analysis

Figure 14

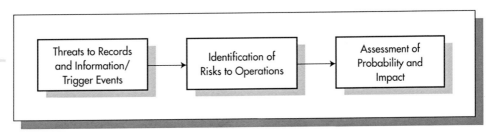

Although in the event-based risk assessment methodology, managers are assessing the probability and impact of risks arising from a given trigger event(s) or threat(s), they can use the same methodology to assess probability and impact as is used in the records and information requirements risk assessment methodology. A scale of one to five can be used to rank probability and impact on the business, with five representing the most likely/severe, and one the least likely/severe. Example 12 demonstrates how to go about conducting this step. Note that the risk is stated as a combination of the trigger event or threat, its effect on the target records and information, and its impact on the organization.

Example 12: Identifying Risks and Conducting a Probability and Impact Analysis

Step 6: Identify risks and conduct probability and impact analysis.

Risk	Probability Ranking	Impact Ranking
Loss or damage to audit reports because of major system outages caused by a computer virus, leading to failure to comply with legal requirements for retention of audit records	4 (0 if netted out)	5
Loss of confidentiality of audit reports because of theft of computer system resources, leading to reputational risk	4 (0 if netted out)	4
Loss or damage to audit reports because of a fire, leading to operating problems	1 (0 if netted out)	5

The reference to "netting out" in Example 12 refers to giving each risk the same probability ranking. Managers should give each risk the same probability ranking if they are assuming as a given that a particular trigger event or threat will occur and focusing the risk assessment only on mitigating the effects of the threat's occurrence. For example, many business continuity initiatives often focus entirely on reducing the impact of a risk event. If the focus is only on reducing impact, analyzing the probability of a threat materializing is not essential, as the assumption already is that the threat or threats will occur. If this approach is taken, managers should enter the same probability ranking for each threat in order to net out the values for the purposes of calculating the risk profile and overall priority profile (e.g., use zero or five in all cases) later on.

Assessing risk proximity, which refers to the timing and duration of the risk, often is particularly important when conducting an event-based risk assessment. The reason is that the level of risk is often time sensitive. For example, the risk of losing most types of vital records is usually considered high in only the first 18 to 24 months of the records' existence. Their criticality decreases over time, with notable exceptions such as legal contracts.[84] As a result, the risk assessment should indicate the time frame in which the risk and its impact will exist.

Key Learning Points
- Step 6 entails assessing the probability and impact of risks arising from given trigger events or threats.
- Assessing probability is not necessary if the focus of the risk assessment is on reducing the impact of a trigger event or threat once it has occurred.
- The same procedures used to assess probability and impact for the requirements-based methodology can be used to complete this step for event-based risk assessment.
- Include an assessment of risk proximity, or the time frame in which the risk and its impact will last, as part of the analysis undertaken at this step.

Steps 7 and 8: Perform Risk Calculations

As in the requirements-based methodology, steps 6 and 7 of the event-based methodology express the results of the risk assessment in numeric terms. Although these

[84] Jones and Keyes, *Emergency Management for Records and Information Management Programs*, 22.

numbers have no inherent significance, they can be useful for making comparisons about the levels of risk associated with different types of records and information or a single record and information type over time, as well as in setting priorities for risk treatment strategies.

Use the formula in Figure 15 to calculate the risk profile for a particular category of records and information.

**Event-Based
Methodology
Risk Profile
Formula**

Figure 15

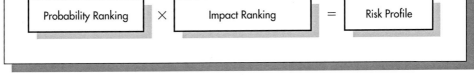

If steps 1 through 3 have been carried out, use the formula in Figure 16 to calculate the overall priority profile for the target records and information.

**Event-Based
Methodology
Overall Risk
Priority Profile
Formula**

Figure 16

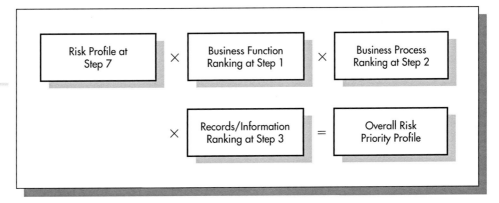

Key Learning Points

- Steps 7 and 8 express the results of the risk assessment in numeric terms.
- Although these numbers have no inherent significance, they can be useful in making comparisons of levels of risk for different record and information types or over time for a single record and information type and in setting priorities for risk treatment.
- Steps 1 through 3 must be completed in order to calculate the overall priority profile.

Step 9: Use the Assessment Results

Once the risk assessment is completed, the results are ready to use to better manage the organization's records and information risks by identifying the types of changes that need to be made, implementing these changes, and monitoring their effectiveness.

If the assessment was focused on a particular type of record or information, or a specific type of threat, the changes naturally will focus only on the target record and information or threat.

Several risk treatment strategies are available for bringing the level of risk within acceptable levels. However, if a range of threats and their probability of

Key Learning Points

- Step 9 entails using the results of the risk assessment to manage the organization's records and information risks.
- Risk treatment strategies will be limited to types that focus on reducing the impact of a trigger event or threat once it occurs if managers have not assessed the probability of the occurrence of a trigger event or threat.
- The results of the risk assessment should be used to develop appropriate risk treatment strategies as part of existing risk management programs or initiatives, and implementation and effectiveness of the strategies should be monitored and tracked.

occurring have not been identified, the focus will be limited to reducing the impact of the risk event once it takes place rather than taking steps to reduce the likelihood that it will occur.

The results of the risk assessment should be incorporated into a business continuity plan, an IT security plan, or other related program, as appropriate, and the implementation and effectiveness of agreed risk treatment strategies should be managed and tracked.

Further Readings

The books and articles presented in this appendix deal with the topic of risk management. Most of the cited items are business-oriented and have practical implications for information professionals. Recent publications are emphasized. These readings are illustrative rather than comprehensive. Some of the works cited here contain extensive bibliographies with many additional references. An extensive amount of literature of a general nature on the subject of records and information risk management does not currently exist.

Two recent works that address the subject of records and information risk management are Barry J. Terenna, CRM, "Risky Business: Proactive Strategies Help Reduce Records-Related Risks," *InfoPro* 3, no.1 (March 2001): 25, and Robert Meagher, "The IM Building Blocks," *The Information Management Journal* 36, no. 1 (January/February 2002): 26, which identifies risk management as one of several critical program building blocks. The interview with Peter W. Morriss, Global Head of Information Risk Management, and Andrew Street, Partner, Technology Assurance Services, KPMG, in Pamella Shimmell, *The Universe of Risk* (Edinburgh Gate, Harlow: Pearson Education Ltd., 2002), also covers the subject of information risk.

The available literature on the subject of records and information risk management often focuses on disaster preparedness and business continuity planning or legal risks. One exception is Anne R. Kenney et al., "Preservation Risk Management for Web Resources," *D-Lib Magazine* 8, no. 1 (January 2002). Available at www.dlib.org/january02/kenney/01kenney.html. For more information on the topic of disaster-related risks, see Kenneth N. Myers, *Manager's Guide to Contingency Planning for Disasters*, Second Edition (New York: John Wiley & Sons, 1999), and Virginia A. Jones and Kris E. Keyes, *Emergency Management for Records and Information Programs* (Prairie Village, KS: ARMA International, 2001).

Much has been written on legal risks and considerations associated with records and information management. Donald S. Skupsky, J.D., *Legal Requirements of Business*

Records (Englewood, CO: Information Requirements Clearing House, 1998) provides a comprehensive guide to regulatory requirements. On the subject of potential legal risks in relation to electronic records management is Rae N. Cogar, J.D., "Exposing Legal Land Mines," *The Information Management Journal* 36, no.1, (January/February 2002): 60, and a number of articles by John C. Montaña, J.D., including "Viruses and the Law: Why the Law is Ineffective," *The Information Management Journal* 34, no. 4 (October 2000): 57, and "Developments in the Law of Electronic Commerce," *The Information Management Journal* 34, no. 1 (January 2000): 52.

The general literature on risk management is much more extensive than that specifically dealing with records and information-related risks. Andrew Holmes' *Risk Management* (Oxford: Capstone Publishing, 2002) offers a tidy summary of basic risk management concepts and some topical risk management issues. For a fascinating history of the development of the science of risk management, see Peter L. Bernstein, *Against the Gods: The Remarkable Story of Risk* (New York: John Wiley & Sons, 1998). The United Kingdom Office of Government Commerce has issued *Management of Risk: Guidance for Practitioners* (London: The Stationary Office, 2002), which contains useful information of a general nature about risk management, including descriptions of risk management tools and their uses as well as a discussion of the management of project-related risks. Christopher L. Culp, *The Risk Management Process* (New York: John Wiley & Sons, 2001), provides an excellent overview of all aspects of risk management while placing emphasis on risk management as being integral to general management and as a value optimizing tool. Michel Crouhy, Dan Galai, and Robert Market, *Risk Management* (New York: McGraw-Hill, 2001), though written primarily from a financial risk management perspective, also touches upon general areas of risk management from a perspective that strongly advocates an integrated approach. Finally, Peter C. Young and Steven C. Tippins, *Managing Business Risk: An Organization-Wide Approach to Risk Management* (New York: AMACOM, 2001), have written an easy-to-follow text on the basics of risk management. Young and Tippin's book also contains useful information on risk simulations (see pages 101-109). David Loader, *Controls, Procedures and Risk* (Oxford: Butterworth-Heinemann Finance, 2002), focuses on operational risk management and contains useful sections on using workflow analysis to identify underlying causes of risk.

For the cost-benefit aspects of risk management, see William Saffady, *Cost Analysis Concepts and Methods for Records Management Projects* (Prairie Village, KS: ARMA International, 1998); Virginia A. Jones and Kris Keyes' *Emergency Management for Records and Information Management Programs* (Prairie Village, KS: ARMA International, 2001); A. Boardman, D. Greenberg, and D. Vining, *Cost-Benefit Analyses: Concepts and Practice*, 2d ed. (Upper Saddle River, New Jersey: Prentice Hall, 2001), and Howard Kunreuther, Chris Cyr, Patricia Grossi, and Wendy Tao, "Using Cost-Benefit Analysis to Evaluate Mitigation for Lifeline Systems," which contains useful case studies demonstrating how to conduct a cost-benefit analysis specifically to choose between risk mitigation strategies aimed at reducing the impact of natural disasters. Available at http://grace.wharton.upenn.edu/risk/wp/wplist01.html.

A number of standards on risk management are available. Standards Australia, Standard AS/NZS 4360:1999, *Risk Management,* presents a generic guide to the establishment and management of risk management practices involving the identification, analysis, evaluation, treatment, communication, and ongoing monitoring of risks. It may be obtained at www.standards.com.au. The British Standards Institute (BSI) has produced PD 6668:2000, *Managing Risk for Corporate Governance,* relating to the management of strategic risks. It outlines a management framework for identifying the threats, determining the risks, implementing and maintaining control measures, and finally reporting on the organization's commitment to the process. In addition, British standard BS 7799, published in two parts—BS 7799-2:2002, *Specification for Information Security Management,* and ISO/IEC 17799:2000, *Information Technology—Code of Practice for Information Security Management—* provides a comprehensive set of controls comprising best practices in information security. To obtain a copy of BSI standards, contact the BSI Group at www.bsi-global.com/index.xalter. Obtain ISO and other international standards at www.iso.org. The UK Institute of Risk Management (IRM), The Association of Insurance and Risk Managers (AIRMIC), and ALARM The National Forum for Risk Management in the Public Sector, have developed a United Kingdom *Risk Management Standard* (London: AIRMIC, ALARM, IRM, 2002) that sets out a comprehensive framework for risk management that is particularly strong on aspects of risk administration. This standard is available at www.airmic.com. ISO has produced ISO/IEC Guide 73:2002, *Risk Management—Vocabulary—Guidelines for Use in Standards,* which will be of help to those needing to develop standardized definitions. This guide may be purchased at www.iso.org.

Glossary

absolute risk: The probability and impact of a risk without taking existing controls into consideration.

consequence: The estimated severity of a risk once it has occurred.

corrective controls: A risk mitigation strategy aimed at reducing the impact of a risk.

direct costs: The direct result of a threat acting on an asset.

hedging: The use of financial arrangements to offset losses that may occur as a result of one risk against losses associated with another risk to neutralize the level of risk.

impact: *See* consequence.

indirect costs: The result of direct damage caused by a threat, although the financial consequences are not as a direct result of the threat.

information: Data that have been organized, analyzed, and interpreted.

key risk indicators: Absolute or relative measures of the organization's tolerance to risk that can be used to signal whether levels of risk have exceeded the organization's risk tolerance level.

managed risk: The probability and impact of the risk when due consideration is given to the controls already in place.

preventative control: A risk mitigation strategy aimed at reducing the likelihood of a risk.

probability: The likelihood or the chance that a risk will occur.

qualitative risk measurement: A method of ranking the probability and impact of risk based on subjective assessment of relevant factors. It can be expressed in words (e.g., high, medium, or low) or numerically (e.g., 1, 2, or 3).

quantitative risk measurement: A method of ranking the probability and impact of a risk based on quantifiable indicators such as cost, or the value of the resources that would be lost if the risk were to occur.

records: Recorded information, regardless of medium or characteristics, made or received by an organization that is evidence of its operations and has value requiring its retention for a specific period of time.

records and information risk: Any risk to the business (e.g., failure to achieve strategic objectives, capitalize on opportunities, or financial loss) arising from some inadequacy in an organization's records and information.

records and information risk management: The management of any risk to the business arising from some inadequacy in an organization's records and information.

residual risk: *See* managed risk.

risk: A thing, event, or action that has not yet occurred, which has a certain probability of occurring and, having occurred, will have a consequence or impact, whether that impact is the outcome of missed opportunity or due to a threat.

risk classification: The process of developing a structured model to categorize risk and fitting observable risk attributes and events into the model.

risk event: A description of an event that poses a risk.

risk financing: Generally refers to a risk mitigation strategy aimed at insuring against the costs associated with the occurrence of a risk event.

risk management: A systematic undertaking that involves assessing and addressing various risks to organizational activities.

risk measurement: The quantification of certain risk exposures for the purpose of comparison to organizational risk tolerances.[85]

risk pooling: All costs are absorbed at the corporate level.

risk proximity: The timing and duration of the threat of a risk.

risk register: A log that contains information on all identified risks.

risk sharing: A practice in which costs are allocated back to the business in proportion to the level of risks generated.

risk tolerance level: The maximum exposure to risk, whether for a given type of risk or across all exposures, that is acceptable, based on the benefits and costs involved.

transferring risk: The process of passing risk along to a third party such as an external service provider.

worry radius: *See* risk tolerance level.

---

[85] This definition is adapted from the definition of risk measurement offered in Culp, *The Risk Management Process*, 211.

Sample Risk Assessment Worksheet— Requirements-Based Approach

Records and Information Risk Assessment Worksheet

Completed By: Date:

Business Function Name: Business Function Ranking:

Business Process Name: Business Process Ranking:

Records/Information Type: Records/Information Ranking:

PART A: Requirements Risk Assessment

Quality	Quality Ranking	Satisfaction Ranking	Effectiveness Rating

Total:

Risks	Related Risks	Impact Ranking	Probability Ranking

Total:

Quality Level and Risk Profile:

Overall Priority Profile:

PART B: Risk Control

Quality	Source of Risk	Risk Control Strategy	Responsibility	Target Date	Current Status

Instructions for Completion

Complete one worksheet for each record/information type

Business Function Name: Input data from Step 1
Business Function Ranking: Input data from Step 1
Business Process Name: Input data from Step 2
Business Process Ranking: Input data from Step 2
Records and Information Type: Input data from Step 3
Records and Information Ranking: Input data from Step 3

Quality: Input data from Step 3
Quality Ranking: Input data from Step 3
Satisfaction Ranking: Input data from Step 4
Effectiveness Rating: Input data from Step 5
Total: Input sum of effectiveness ratings for all record qualities

Risks: Input data from Step 6 on the types of risks arising from gaps in quality
Related Risks: Input data from Step 6

Impact Ranking: Input data from Step 6
Probability Ranking: Input data from Step 6
Total: Input data from Step 6

Quality Level and Risk Profile: Input data from Step 7
Overall Priority Profile: Input data from Step 8
Quality: Input data from Step 3
Source of Risk: Input data from Step 4 and/or Step 6
Risk Control Strategy: Input data from Step 9
Responsibility: Identify the person responsible for implementing the risk control strategy
Target Date: Input expected date for implementation of the risk control strategy
Current Status: Input current implementation status and keep current

Sample Risk Assessment Worksheet— Event-Based Approach

Records and Information Risk Assessment Worksheet

Completed By: Date:

Business Function Name: Business Function Ranking:

Business Process Name: Business Process Ranking:

Records/Information Type: Records/Information Ranking:

PART A: Event-Based Risk Assessment

Trigger Event/Threat	Risks	Proximity	Probability Rating	Impact Rating

Total:

Risk Profile:

Overall Priority Profile:

PART B: Risk Control

Trigger Event/Threat	Risk Control Strategy	Responsibility	Target Date	Current Status

Instructions for Completion

Complete one worksheet for each record/information type

Business Function Name: Input data from Step 1
Business Function Ranking: Input data from Step 1
Business Process Name: Input data from Step 2
Business Process Ranking: Input data from Step 2
Records and Information Type: Input data from Step 3
Records and Information Ranking: Input data from Step 3

Trigger Event/Threats: Input data from Step 4
Risks: Input data from Step 4
Proximity: Input data from Step 4
Probability Rating: Input data from Step 6
Impact Rating: Input data from Step 6

Risk Profile: Input data from Step 7
Overall Priority Profile: Input data from Step 8

Trigger Event/Threat: Input data from Step 4
Risk Control Strategy: Input data from Step 9, drawing on data from Step 5 as well
Responsibility: Identify the person responsible for implementing the risk control strategy
Target Date: Input expected date for implementation of the risk control strategy
Current Status: Input current implementation status and keep current

About the Author

Victoria L. Lemieux is a UK-based records and information management specialist with over fifteen years of extensive practical experience in a variety of sectors. She has held management positions in the public sector, academia, and financial services. Parallel with her administrative work, she has undertaken consulting assignments for international agencies, such as the Commonwealth Secretariat, the UN, and the World Bank, as well as a number of private and public sector entities in Canada, the Caribbean, Africa, and the UK.

She is a graduate of the University of Toronto and the University of British Columbia (Master of Archival Studies Program) and holds a doctorate in Archives Studies from University College London. She has lectured on archives and records management at the University of Alberta and the University of the West Indies.

Ms. Lemieux is also a frequent speaker at conferences and seminars and has published extensively. Her publications include *Better Information Practices: Improving Records and Information Management in the Public Service* (London: Commonwealth Secretariat, 1999) and *Management of Public Sector Records Series: Business Systems Analysis* (London: International Records Management Trust, 2000). Contact details: vicki.lemieux@ntlworld.com.

About the Association

ARMA International is the leading professional organization for persons in the expanding field of records and information management.

As of May 2004, ARMA has about 10,000 members in the United States, Canada, and 37 other countries around the world. Within the United States, Canada, New Zealand, Japan, Jamaica, and Singapore, ARMA has nearly 150 local chapters that provide networking and leadership opportunities through monthly meetings and special seminars.

ARMA's mission is to provide education, research, and networking opportunities to information professionals, to enable them to use their skills and experience to leverage the value of records, information, and knowledge as corporate assets and as contributors to organizational success.

The ARMA International headquarters office is located in Lenexa, Kansas, in the Kansas City metropolitan area. Office hours are 8:30 A.M. to 5:00 P.M., Central Time, Monday through Friday.

ARMA International
13725 W. 109th St., Ste. 101
Lenexa, Kansas 66215
800.422.2762 • 913.341.3808
Fax: 913.341.3742
hq@arma.org
www.arma.org